ON GOD
AND POLITICAL DUTY

The Library of Liberal Arts
OSKAR PIEST, FOUNDER

ON GOD AND POLITICAL DUTY

JOHN CALVIN

Edited, with an Introduction, by
JOHN T. MCNEILL

. . . .
The Library of Liberal Arts
published by
ITT Bobbs-Merrill Educational Publishing Company, Inc.
Indianapolis

John Calvin: 1509-1564

Second Edition
Eighteenth printing—1985

Library of Congress Catalog Card Number: 50-4950
ISBN: 0-672-60184-2 (pbk.)

CONTENTS

SELECTED BIBLIOGRAPHY   vi

EDITOR'S INTRODUCTION   vii

NOTE ON THE EDITION   xxvi

ON GOD AND POLITICAL DUTY

Selections from

I.   Institutes of the Christian Religion
     Dedication to Francis I   3
     On Christian Liberty   26
     On Civil Government   44

II. Commentaries on the Epistle of Paul the
     Apostle to the Romans   83

III. Commentaries on the Book of the
     Prophet Daniel   88

SELECTED BIBLIOGRAPHY

CALVIN'S WORKS

Joannis Calvini opera quae supersunt omnia. Fifty-nine volumes. Brunswick, 1863-1900 (*Corpus Reformatorum series*).

Joannis Calvini opera selecta. Edited by Peter Barth and Wilhelm Niesel. Five volumes. Munich, 1926-36.

Commentaries. Forty-five volumes. Edinburgh, 1844-55. Republished with new introductions. Grand Rapids, 1947-.

Institutes of the Christian Religion. Translated from the Latin and collated with the author's last edition in French, by John Allen (1813). Two volumes. Philadelphia, 1945.

Tracts Relating to the Reformation. Translated by Henry Beveridge. Three volumes. Edinburgh, 1844-51.

COLLATERAL READING

Baron, Hans, "Calvinist Republicanism and its Historical Roots," *Church History,* VIII (1939), 30-42.

Bohatec, Josef, *Calvins Lehre von Staat und Kirche.* Breslau, 1937.

Breen, Quirinus, *John Calvin: a Study in French Humanism.* Grand Rapids, 1932.

Carlyle, R. W. and A. H. Carlyle, *A History of Political Theory in the West.* Volume VI. Edinburgh, 1926.

Chenevière, Marc-Edouard, *La pensée politique de Calvin.* Geneva, 1937.

Doumergue, Emile, *Jean Calvin, les hommes et les choses de son temps.* Seven volumes. Lausanne, 1899-1927.

Foster, Herbert Darling, *Collected Papers of Herbert Darling Foster.* Hanover, N. H., 1929.

Gloede, Günther, *Theologia naturalis bei Calvin.* Stuttgart, 1934.

Hunt, R. N. Carew, "Calvin's Theory of the State," *Church Quarterly Review,* CVIII (1929), 56-71.

McNeill, John T., "Natural Law in the Teaching of the Reformers," *Journal of Religion,* XXVI (1946), 168-82.

————"Thirty Years of Calvin Study," *Church History,* XVII (1948), 207-40.

————"The Democratic Element in Calvin's Thought," *Church History,* XVIII (1949), 153-41.

Mesnard, Pierre, *L'essor de la philosophie politique au XVIᵉ siècle en France.* Paris, 1936.

Murray, Robert H., *Political Consequences of the Reformation.* London, 1926.

INTRODUCTION

True wisdom, says John Calvin at the beginning of his *Institutes,* consists in the knowledge of God and of ourselves. God is to be known in his work of creation and redemption. He is revealed inadequately through nature and reason, adequately and authoritatively through the Scriptures, which are his authentic utterance. He is clothed with majesty and sovereign power, yet "he allures us to himself by his mercy." Man, enfeebled by sin, rises to his true life by God's undeserved grace, and finds his liberty in a voluntary obedience to God. Throughout his writings Calvin stresses his unwavering belief that the high Sovereign of the universe is also intimately present in the world of mankind. He sees God's hand in all historical events, and never doubts that in our personal affairs and choices we have "dealings with God" all the days of our life (*"in tota vita negotium cum Deo"*).

We cannot understand the political element in Calvin's teaching, any more than in the teaching of St. Paul or St. Augustine, without being aware that it hangs upon his scriptural conception of the relation of God to man and of the consequent obligation of man to man. He has numerous points in common both with Aquinas and with Marsiglio; but he is less indebted to Aristotle and more insistently scriptural than either of these contrasting medieval interpreters of government.

The dealings with God to which Calvin refers include far more than acts of worship and contemplation. The Calvinist piety embraces all the day-by-day concerns of life, in family and neighborhood, education and culture, business and politics. These are for Calvin realms of duty in which men ought so to act as to honor God and benefit their fellows.

vii

Calvin's awe-stricken consciousness of God carries with it no indifference to mundane matters. Rather it demands the most intense participation in the common affairs of men. If, in Aristotle's phrase, man is a "political animal," he is in Calvin's view not less but more political when he is motivated by religion. Calvin is repelled, and even appalled by the type of sectarian spirituality that would desert the sphere of politics as beneath the spiritual man's plane of living. More emphatically than most theologians, he calls for active and positive political behavior.

I

Calvin wrote no extended formal treatise on government. His utterances on the subject are incidental, but they represent a continuous, thoughtful interest in political matters. The extracts here given are from writings scattered over a period of about twenty-five years. In the first of these he is addressing the greatest monarch of his time. In the last he is applying principles of political duty to a royal figure portrayed in an Old Testament book. He shows in the other selections political interests that go far beyond the topic of kingly authority and duty. His own age, and his immediate environment in Geneva, offered for consideration the phenomena of government by elective assemblies. Calvin is not so naïve as to suppose that political salvation comes from the adoption of any mere structure of government, but his decided preference is for some type of government in which citizens in general share responsibility.

"Shakespeare loves a king," but Calvin rarely mentions one with admiration. It is true that in passages of his works he shows a high regard for biblical kings who are approved by the Scripture writers. His warmest praise of King David is associated, however, with his belief that David was the author of that matchless treasury of devotion, the Book of Psalms. His approach to contemporary kings was respectful but far from subservient; he always assumes the rôle of a counsellor rather than of a mere suppliant. He wrote numerous letters to the crowned heads of nations and to others in positions of power, seeking to move them to adopt a tolerant attitude toward their Protestant subjects, or urging them to action in the reform of the Church in their domains. The earliest and most notable of these is the letter to Francis I of France, which serves as an introduction to the *Institutes of the Christion Religion*. It was written in August 1535. The first edition of this work was then about to go to the Basel printer, Thomas Platter; it appeared in March of the following year.

The letter offers a defense of the French Protestant minority, then subjected to persecution, against the charges of heresy and sedition. Early in the document we come upon statements of Calvin's fundamental ideas concerning the duties of kings, and in fact of all who bear rule. It belongs to true royalty for a king to acknowledge himself "the minister of God." Where the glory of God is not the end of government there is no legitimate sovereignty, but usurpation. The Kingship of Christ is over all earthly dominion. One is reminded here of a celebrated passage in Augustine's *City of God* (v. 24), oft quoted by medieval authors and known as the "Mirror of Princes," where the great African Father observes that in the Christian view those emperors are happy who "make their power the handmaid of God's majesty."

The significance of this letter lies not only in its vehement defense of the cause to which Calvin was attached and assertion of its right to the King's recognition, but also in the fact that the young scholar ventured thus boldly to admonish the proud and absolute monarch of a great nation. Aroused by the sufferings of his fellow believers, Calvin charges with "falsehoods, artifices, and calumnies" the inspirers of persecution who have gained influence over the King. He derives his munitions from the arsenal of Scripture and from the writings of the Church Fathers. His attack is merciless; it is with no tolerant spirit that he demands toleration. By implication the King himself is involved in the denunciation of the policy of "extermination" which the government of France has apparently instituted. We do not know that Francis ever saw the letter; if he did, his policy was not affected by it. Calvin's passionate vehemence was less likely to be effective than a more moderate plea might have been. There were more prudent and balanced statements within the book itself in which we discern the outlines of his political doctrine. But the letter to Francis gave startling evidence that Calvin and his followers regarded all rulers as subject to criticism from the standpoint of scriptural religion.

II

Two chapters are here given from the final Latin edition (1559) of the *Institutes,* in John Allen's translation. Substantially the first of these texts is contained in the final chapter of the 1536 edition.[1] Calvin was about twenty-six years old when he completed the writing of the first edition, but his thought was already so mature in this field that he found little occasion to alter or expand this passage in his later editions. The same statements hold for the second selection, with the qualification that considerable additional matter of some interest was introduced, chiefly in the last edition. The structure of the work as a whole was materially altered in the series of revisions, and it was extended to five times its original size. While in the first edition the two topics here treated were separated only by a section on "ecclesiastical power," they appear in separate books of the final edition, and the materials inserted between them comprise no less than twenty-five chapters. Moreover, these are now set in different main divisions of the treatise. Despite the fact that in the enlarged *Institutes* our two selections have been widely

---

[1] Chapter VI: *"De libertate christiana, potestate ecclesiastica et politica administratione."* In Peter Barth's edition, *Joannis Calvini opera selecta,* Volume I (Munich, 1926), this long chapter occupies pages 223-280.

separated and placed under different general headings,[2] they still bear references to one another, and the student will do well to remember that in their original form the relationship between them was made obvious in the organization of the work.

In the chapter on liberty, Calvin is largely concerned with the topic of conscience. Man stands helpless before the divine law, since the law condemns all imperfections. From this unhappy state God calls men "with paternal gentleness" into the liberty of faith. Man's good actions arise in glad response to this call, as children respond to a kind father. All the good works of the patriarchs referred to in the Epistle to the Hebrews are there said to be done through faith. It is important that we should be aware that we have liberty of choice with regard to external matters of the class of *adiaphora,* things morally indifferent. If this assurance is lacking, conscience may be entrapped into a course of meaningless cumulative self-punishment, and be led to despair. Yet for Calvin the things indifferent are not to be used in ways that escape moral restraint. Ivory and gold, music, good food and wine are to be enjoyed without excess and without pride or covetousness. Christian liberty is thus opposed both to unwholesome asceticism and to irresponsible indulgence. It requires that, like St. Paul, we shall know "how to be abased and how to abound," and that we avoid offending the scruples of others. It may involve, for example, abstinence from flesh on Fridays in deference to our neighbor's conscience.

Thus conscience is by no means merely an individual matter; it must be exercised with consideration for other men's consciences, where no imperative duty is thereby infringed. On the other hand, we must not by yielding too much "for-

2 Book III of this edition, in which our chapter "On Christian Liberty" appears, is entitled: "On the Manner of Receiving the Grace of Christ, the Benefits which we Derive from It, and the Effects which Follow It." Book IV, which concludes with the chapter "On Civil Government," bears the title: "The True Church, and the Necessity of Our Union with Her, Being the Mother of All the Pious."

tify the conscience of our neighbor in sin." Calvin's rule is that we are to assert or restrict our liberty in accordance with charity and a due regard for the welfare of our neighbor (*studendum charitati et spectanda proximi aedificatio*, III, xix, 12).

Calvin here introduces the question of obligation to political authority. He warns against the error of supposing that since the Christian's conscience is set free by faith, he may disregard this obligation. But man stands under a double government (*duplex in homine regimen*, III, xix, 15): spiritual and political; these require to be separately considered. He first examines in connection with "spiritual government" the meaning of the word conscience, "a kind of medium between God and man," which "places man before the Divine tribunal." He insists on the principle that conscience, in the strict sense of the term, is directed to God, not to human laws. The nature of obligation to public law and government concerns the relations among men on the temporal level, which are discussed later, in Book IV, chapter xx.

III

This chapter (IV, xx) is Calvin's most systematic statement on government, and summarizes his entire thought on the subject. Again he distinguishes the two realms, of the spiritual and the temporal, and confines the liberty of the Gospel to the former. On the other hand, he protests against the notion that civil government is a polluted thing with which Christians have nothing to do. The political state has, indeed, functions directly connected with religion. It protects and supports the worship of God, promotes justice and peace, and is a necessary aid in our earthly pilgrimage toward heaven—as necessary as bread and water, light and air, and more excellent in that it makes possible the use of these, and secures higher blessings to men. Calvin is eloquent on the benefits of government in combatting offenses against religion, securing tranquility, safeguarding private property, promoting honesty and other virtues, and maintaining "a public form of religion among Christians and humanity among men."

The State is not free to dictate laws to the Church, but is obligated to protect it. There is common ground here between Calvin and St. Thomas Aquinas; but Calvin gives to the State as over against the Church a somewhat larger sphere of action than the medieval doctor, and in this approaches more nearly to the position of Dante in *De Monarchia,* if not to that of a Marsiglio in the *Defensor Pacis.* Marsiglio has been regarded (though I believe unjustly) as a prophet of secularism. Certainly Calvin is not that. In his warm admiration for political government, he does not for a moment regard it as a realm of mere secularity. It is God-given, a "benevolent provision" for man's good, and for it men should give God thanks. The function of the magistrate is a "sacred ministry," and to regard it as incompatible with religion is an insult to God. Calvin has here in mind the Anabaptists and other enthusiastic groups. When he wrote, the fanatical experiment of the Münster Anabaptists had very recently come to a tragic close.

Calvin insists on applying this teaching to all sorts of political rulers. Paul, writing under the least satisfactory kind of government which is "by one man" and accompanied by a "common servitude," states that "there is no power but of God." It is evident that Calvin regards even non-Christian governments and governors as divinely authorized and worthy of obedience. A state may be well constituted though it "neglects the polity of Moses" and rests upon the common law of nations. Yet he is addressing Christian rulers and subjects of professedly Christian states, and is of course primarily concerned with politics in a Christian setting.

Magistrates are the guardians of the laws, and their very making and enforcement of law is "presided over" by God. Theirs is a holy calling, "the most sacred and honorable" of all. In a powerful passage it is pointed out that their realization of this should induce them to pursue zealously clemency,

justice, and other virtues becoming to their office. Calvin admonishes them as "vicegerents of God" to avoid bribery, to
defend good men from injury, to aid the oppressed, vindicate
the innocent, and justly to mete out punishment and reward. They are obligated where necessary to suppress violence by force. The commandment not to kill does not bind
the justice of God of which they are executors. But there
must not be undue severity. No equitable sentence is pronounced without mercy, yet an ill-advised lenity toward violent men may prove cruelty to the many who become their
victims. By the same principle, a war of defense against a
ruthless aggressor may become a necessary duty, though only
when every peaceable effort has failed. Against this necessity
frontier garrisons, foreign alliances, and military preparations are legitimate precautionary measures.

Calvin realizes that government requires revenues and taxa-
tion. These funds are not the ruler's private incomes but belong to the people; they are in fact the very blood of the
people and should be used in their behalf as a sacred trust,
and not collected with rapacity or wasted in luxury.

IV

The treatment of the duties of magistracy is followed by a
discussion of public law. Calvin, a doctor of law, was at home
in this field, but he restrains himself from a lengthy disquisi-
tion and handles the topic succinctly, with primary reference
to the Old Testament. He follows the traditional distinction
of the "moral, ceremonial, and judicial" aspects of the Mosaic
law, of which the first only is of perpetual authority. The
judicial law supplied a political constitution with rules of
equity and justice by which men might dwell together in
peace. The ceremonial law aided piety in the childhood stage
of the development of the Jewish nation. Valuable as these
were, they were of passing necessity. Only the moral law en-
dures without change. It is summarized in the Ten Commandments, and in the Commandment of Love (Leviticus

19:18; Deuteronomy 6:5; Matthew 22:37-39). Nations are free to adopt such laws as they may find expedient, without regard to the political constitution, or judicial law, of ancient Israel, but always on the principles of the moral law and "the perpetual rule of love."

At many points in his other writings Calvin has touched upon the topic of natural law and equity, but his references here to this vital theme are disappointingly compressed. In his *Commentary on Romans* (1:21-22; 2:14-15) he affirms that God has set in all men's minds a knowledge of himself—"his eternity, power, goodness, truth, righteousness, and mercy." Gentiles, though they have in large degree disregarded these intimations of a divine natural morality, have nevertheless, "without a monitor," devised laws which reflect it.

It is beyond doubt that there are naturally inborn (*ingenitas*) in the minds of men certain conceptions of justice and uprightness, which the Greeks call "anticipations" (προλήψεις). They have therefore a law without the law [and] are not altogether lacking in knowledge of right and equity. [St. Paul] has set nature over against the written law, understanding that for the Gentiles a natural light of justice shines, which supplies the place of the law by which the Jews are instructed; so that they are "a law unto themselves." [3]

In an earlier passage of the *Institutes,* Calvin gives an extended treatment of the moral law as expressed in the Ten Commandments. He there refers to that "interior law . . . imprinted on the heart of everyone," which in some sense conveys the teaching of the Commandments. The inner monitor that expresses this is conscience, which ever and anon arouses us from moral sleep. The written moral law of the Bible is given by God to attest and clarify the precepts of natural law, and fix them in the memory (II, viii, 1).

In the present context we have a variant expression of the same teaching. Calvin's words are:

[3] In this Introduction, the translations of quotations from Calvin's works are by the writer.

Now since it is a fact that the Law of God which we call "moral" is nothing else than a testimony of the natural law and of that conscience which has been engraven by God in the minds of men, the entire scheme (ratio) of this equity has been prescribed in it (IV, xx, 16).

Thus Calvin adopts, and clearly enunciates, the traditional view that a primal natural law has been imparted by God to all men, and that the scriptural Commandments bear witness to it (naturalis legis testimonium). All such laws as men may frame in accordance with the natural law, however they may diverge from those of other states, and from the Jewish law, are to be approved. The Laws of Moses were not all intended for all nations; they took account of the "peculiar circumstances" of the Hebrew people. The Commandments are, so to speak, a divine transcription for the Jewish people of the natural law that has always and everywhere been lodged in men's hearts, and properly governs all enacted laws.[4]

In general Calvin identifies natural law with equity. He seems to think of equity not in the technical sense of the human modification, in given circumstances, of the letter of a written code, but in the popular sense of common justice. Equity is natural, and hence "the same for all mankind"; and all laws should "have equity for their end." It is noteworthy that both Luther and Melanchthon, who were not trained in law, use the technical language and make equity a "mitigation" of the summum ius, the limit of the law, while Calvin, the trained lawyer, avoids a definition of the term and gives it a sense virtually as inclusive as that of natural law itself. He leaves us, however, in no doubt of his desire to emphasize the normative authority of natural in relation to positive law. In all this Calvin has no notion of modern secular interpretations of natural law. It is a part of the divine endowment of the natural man, impaired indeed, but

[4] For further evidence see the present writer's article, "Natural Law in the Teaching of the Reformers," The Journal of Religion, XXVI (1946), 179ff.

not obliterated by sin, evident in common concepts of justice and in the inner voice of conscience.

Calvin's affirmation of law, on this basis, is accompanied by a justification of participation in its judicial processes. An injured person has the right to claims its protection, and bring his cause before the courts. The magistrate in legal judgments exercises "a holy gift of God," and litigation is to be sought without feelings of revenge or enmity. St. Paul asserted his rights as a Roman citizen, and his rebuke of the Christians of Corinth (I Cor. 6) was designed to check their spirit of dissension and covetousness. Again he invokes the rule of charity, which is not necessarily violated when we defend our property.

V

Calvin lays emphasis repeatedly upon the duty of obedience to magistrates as vicegerents of God. So far as the individual citizen is concerned, this rule of obedience applies even to tyrannical rulers who seem to be in no sense representatives of God. An impious king is thought of as a scourge visited upon a people in punishment for sin; yet he too possesses a divine authority. Old Testament passages are adduced here: Jeremiah represents God as calling Nebuchadnezzar "my servant" and commanding the people to serve him and live, though in fact he was "a pestilent and cruel tyrant." Under a wicked ruler we are not to rebel, but to consider our own sins, and implore the help of God. This is not futile, for God does intervene to lay tyrants low, sometimes raising up leaders who are his appointed instruments of revolution even when they know it not. "Let princes hear and fear!"

The passage here selected from the Commentary on Romans (1539) accords with these views. The magistrate in punishment exercises the vengeance of God against the violation of his Commandments. Calvin remarks that no "private man" may seize the reins of government from the appointed ruler. In paragraphs not included in the selection, he applies to government the principle of charity, which is the fulfillment of the law. To induce anarchy is to violate charity; obedience to magistrates is a great part of charity.

But we create a wholly false impression of Calvin's political ideas if we give sole attention to his exhortations to obedience. It will be observed that in commenting on Romans 13:1, he stresses the point that Paul speaks of the "higher," not of the "highest" power. The ruler has no authority that contends with God's. Calvin frequently reminds us that "we must obey God rather than men" (Acts 5:24). In the last edition of the *Institutes* he reinforces this argument (in the final paragraph of the work) by fresh Bible texts: in Daniel 6:22 the king has abrogated (*abrogaverit*) his authority by raising his hand against God; and Hosea 5:11 condemns the submissive obedience of the Israelites to the decrees of Jeroboam II enjoining idolatry. God does not resign his right to mortals when he makes them rulers.

Nor does Calvin deprive subjects of all right of resistance. The classical passage here is in the *Institutes* IV, xx, 31, which is in all editions of the work. So far as private persons are concerned, they are never permitted to resist. But if there are magistrates whose constitutional function is the protection of the people against the license of kings (*populares magistratus ad moderandam regum libidinem*), such as the Ephors of Sparta, the Roman tribunes, or the Demarchs of Athens, or, perhaps with such power as is exercised by the meetings of the Three Estates in the several modern kingdoms, it is not only their right but their duty to oppose the king's violence and cruelty. It would be "nefarious perfidy" for them to fail in this duty, and thus to "betray the liberty of the people."

How should we understand these references to the ancient popular magistrates and to the estates in modern realms? Calvin introduces his reference to the latter with the word "perhaps." This may suggest that he hesitated to regard them, or, at least, to regard all of them, as functioning like the Ephors for the protection of the people against tyranny. He was doubtless aware that the classes of ancient magistrates here mentioned were all elected by popular vote. This was not uniformly the case in the membership of the estates; in some nations it was hardly the case at all. If he possessed detailed knowledge of the estates or parliaments of England, Scotland, Sweden, Denmark, Norway, Poland, Bohemia, Hungary, and Spain, of the diets of the Swiss Confederation and the imperial diets of Germany, he would observe wide differences among them in constitution and function, and in potentiality for defense against monarchical absolutism or tyranny. But Calvin would have in mind primarily his native France, and he could not fail to be aware that the French estates had not even met since three years before his own birth. During his lifetime, any expectation that the Three Estates would redeem France from absolutism was faint indeed. His "perhaps" may be, in relation to France, an expression of doubt regarding the very survival of the institution. Yet it is noteworthy that in all these European organs of quasi representative government he saw at least the possibility of some guarantee of liberty and security for the people. His words were, in fact, an invitation to these bodies to play the rôle of the Ephors and check the irresponsible arrogance of kings.

This emphatic and suggestive passage opened a path for writers like Francis Hotman and the authors of the *Vindiciae contra Tyrannos* who a few years after Calvin's death would frame doctrines of resistance that were to be vastly influential in the practical world. It also gave suggestions to the British seventeenth-century political prophets, Rutherford, Sydney, and Locke. It was not less but more influential in that it came as a concession at the end of a discussion that is anxiously conservative.

VI

That Calvin was hostile to monarchy as a form of government has been affirmed and denied by equally competent scholars.[5] At times he refuses to choose among the forms of government, and he avoids any blanket denunciation of the royal office. The piety of some Bible kings would exclude that. He has, as we saw, a high ideal for the behavior of kings. Good government under a king is for him a possibility. Yet the fact is that he is habitually severe in his judgment of the kings of history and of his own time. This characteristic is most marked after the inception of the severe persecutions of Henry II in France and of Mary in England; but no express connection with these matters appears in his treatment. Denunciations of bad kings who come to notice in the commentaries readily and frequently lead to expressions of unqualified disparagement of kings in general. Calvin's Sermons on Job (1554) and on Deuteronomy (1554-55) offer numerous instances of this. We have included here, chiefly to illustrate the point, selections from his Lectures on Daniel, a work of his later years (1561).

The Book of Daniel, a story of heroic fidelity and divine deliverance, lent itself to treatment by the spokesman and counsellor of the harassed minority of Protestants in France; and Calvin devotes sixty-six lectures to its twelve chapters. The work bears a dedicatory epistle to the pious in France, in which Daniel's "memorable example of incredible constancy" is held before them, along with "the goodness of God at the close of this tragedy."

In these lectures we may sometimes discern an allegory of French affairs of the times. Nebuchadnezzar wishes to

[5] In the pages that follow in this Introduction a few sentences are taken from my article, "The Democratic Element in Calvin's Thought," *Church History*, XVIII (1949), 153-71, and there is a further indebtedness to the materials of that paper. For permission to use these I am indebted to Professor Matthew Spinka, Chairman of the Editorial Board of *Church History*.

have in his kingdom no dissident religious minority. He is blinded by pride: "And to this day we see with what arrogance all earthly monarchs conduct themselves." His officers obey his edicts, since they have no religion but that of their fathers (Lecture xiii). Daniel, Calvin notes, presents in the Babylonian kings a description of the greatness of a royal power exercised not because it is lawful, but by tacit consent of subjects who dare not murmur. Belshazzar fails to learn from the punishment of Nebuchadnezzar's pride (Lecture xxv).

It is Darius who is the type of royal incapacity and misgovernment; yet he is not so bad as modern kings. His initial recognition of virtue in Daniel suggests that "we ought to weep over the heartlessness of kings in these days, who proudly despise God's gift in all good men." We see how unworthy of their power kings usually are. Their favorites are flatterers, panders, and buffoons (Lecture xxvii). Darius yields to the counsels of evil and designing nobles. At each stage of his moral downfall Calvin generalizes on modern kings. "If one could uncover the hearts of kings, he would find hardly one in a hundred who does not despise everything divine" (Lecture xviii). Yielding to wicked persuasion, kings become slaves of their own servants: a prisoner in a dungeon is freer than they. "Thus slaves rule the kingdoms of the world" (Lecture xix). When one has perused many such passages, it is difficult to accept the judgment of those who hold that the Reformer has no hostility toward the monarchical form of government. A growing revulsion toward kingship itself seems to be involved in his persistent, and often sweeping, denunciation of kings.

On the other hand it is manifest that Calvin is anxious to avoid the language of political revolution. He quotes "Honor the King," and observes that it is vain for those who have no part in determining the form of government to dispute about it. Which form is advantageous will depend upon circumstances. But, in the 1543 edition of the *Institutes* he introduced, following this neutral statement, the flat assertion that "aristocracy, or aristocracy tempered by democracy, far excels all other forms." He retained this phrase in the 1559 edition, supporting it on the ground that justice, rectitude, and discernment are rare in kings. He then adds:

The vice or inadequacy of men thus renders it safer and more tolerable that many (*plures*) hold the sway (*gubernacula*), so that they may mutually be helpers to each other, teach and admonish one another, and if one asserts himself unfairly, the many may be censors and masters, repressing his wilfulness (*libidinem*).[6]

Thus Calvin clearly takes his stand upon a plural magistracy as contrasted with a monarchy. There is safety in numbers, who can check the ambition of anyone disposed to seek domination. This, it may be noted, is a reversal of the view of St. Thomas Aquinas, who in *The Governance of Princes* argues for monarchy from the principle of unity (chapter ii), and from the judgment, supported by the example of ancient Rome, that government by the many more often turns into tyranny than government by one (chapter v). In Geneva the scriptural principle of mutual admonition, or "fraternal correction" (cf. 2 Thess. 3:15), in which Calvin here sees a safeguard against arrogance, was incorporated into the constitution of the Church. Moreover, in 1557, Calvin induced the Little Council, the chief organ of civil government, to adopt the practice of a quarterly meeting for mutual criticism "in fraternal charity"; the proceedings of this session were kept secret.

There are other passages that guide us to an understanding of these concise sentences from the *Institutes*. On Romans 13:4 he notes that rulers are "obligated to God and to men." On Micah 5:5 he finds authorization for the popular election of rulers. He takes the word "shepherds" there in the sense of political rulers, and observes:

For the condition of the people most to be desired is that in which they create their shepherds by general vote (*communibus suffragiis*). For when anyone by force usurps the supreme

6 *Institutes*, IV, xx, 8.

power, that is tyranny. And where men are born to king-ship, this does not seem to be in accordance with liberty. Hence the prophet says: we shall set up princes for our-selves; that is, the Lord will not only give the Church free-dom to breathe, but also institute a definite and well-ordered government, and establish this upon the common suffrages of all (*Opera*, in *Corpus Reformatorum* edition, XLIII, 374).

The system here clearly favored is one that rests upon popular election, which is also thought of as the work of God. Without the slightest sense of incongruity, the theocratic and democratic principles are drawn together. The blend of aris-tocracy and democracy that he recommends as superior to all other forms of government should be thought of in the light of this. When he speaks of aristocracy as "the rule of the principal persons" he is in all probability not thinking of any hereditary ruling caste. He sees liberty infringed when kings are born to kingship, and we may assume that the "principal persons" are not such by inheritance, but through the recognition of their qualities by their fellows. It would be perilous, however, to press this point too far. Where a hereditary nobility exists it has some actual authority and influence which ought to be brought to bear for good gov-ernment, and thus entails a specific responsibility. Calvin would have agreed with John Knox—whose political attitude was in general more revolutionary than his—when that Re-former writes:

To bridle the fury and rage of princes in free kingdoms and realms . . . it pertains to the nobility, sworn and born to be councillors of the same, and also to the barons and people, whose votes and consent are to be required in all great and weighty matters of the commonwealth.

VII

Calvin became a citizen of Geneva only after his com-pletion of the last edition of the *Institutes*. He had already committed himself to views consonant with membership in a republic, and had helped to reshape the constitution and

laws of the city. The system of government was that of a
conservative democracy. Calvin's word for democracy (*politia*)
came to him from past ages with suggestions of disorderli-
ness and anarchy which he largely retained, and which in
many European minds still attach to the word "democracy"
itself. He is cautious, therefore, in his use of the term. But
his "aristocracy-democracy" formula is not only consistent
with a republican order of government, but in fact conducive to it. In the commentaries he frequently expresses warm
praise of liberty, and this is sometimes associated with the
right of the people to elect their rulers. Twice in the Homilies
on First Samuel he refers to liberty as an "inestimable good,"
(*Opera*, in *Corpus Reformatorium* edition XXIX, 544, and
XXX, 185); the same language is used in the Commentary on
Jeremiah (XXXIX, 178), and in a reference to Deuteronomy
24:7, liberty is characterized as "more than the half of life"
(XXIV, 628). These sentences from his Sermons on Deuteronomy indicate his wholehearted approval of the elective principle:

When [in the days of the Judges] God gave such a privilege
to the Jews, he ratified thereby his adoption and gave proof
that he had chosen them for his inheritance, and that he
desired that their condition should be better and more excellent than that of their neighbors, where there were kings
and princes but no liberty. . . . If we have the liberty to
choose judges and magistrates, since this is an excellent gift,
let it be preserved and let us use it in good conscience. . . .
If we argue about human governments we can say that to
be in a free state is much better than to be under a prince.
[Disputes of this sort are unprofitable, but:] It is much more
endurable to have rulers who are chosen and elected . . .
and who acknowledge themselves subject to the laws, than
to have a prince who gives utterance without reason. Let
those to whom God has given liberty and freedom (*franchise*)
use it . . . as a singular benefit and a treasure that cannot
be prized enough (XXVII, 410-11; 458-60).

Thus the priceless boon of liberty is to be cherished and
defended; but it is not to be sought by violent revolution,
and not to be expressed in ways that escape the bounds of law.

Calvin's idea of good government is concisely stated:

I readily acknowledge that no kind of government is more happy than this, where liberty is regulated with becoming moderation and properly established on a durable basis (*ad diuturnitatem*).[7]

In February, 1560, on the eve of an election, he addressed the General Assembly of citizens urging them "to choose [their magistrates] with a pure conscience, without regard to anything but the honor and glory of God, for the safety and defense of the republic." Thus theocracy and democracy were easily and naturally associated in his teaching, and impressed by him upon the city-state that was the special sphere of his activity, in which he sought to establish, according to his pattern, a regulated and enduring liberty.

To our modern minds, in Calvin's Geneva the "regulation" outweighed the "liberty." It is idle to estimate the experiment by modern standards; but, at any rate, under the system of governing elective councils, and of annual elections, the constitutional means of revision were maintained. Calvin was no modern man, and he was not writing in the interests of secular conceptions of democracy. Government was for him concerned with what we call the "rights of man" only in relation to scriptural concepts of God, the moral law, and "the perpetual rule of love." But from these presuppositions he reached certain viewpoints that have leavened political theory in modern liberal states. A study of the selections that follow will in some measure enable the reader to grasp these elements of his teaching, and to appreciate their bearing upon the contemporary political problems and interests.

JOHN T. McNEILL

[7] *Institutes*, IV, xx, 8.

NOTE ON THE EDITION

The translation of the *Institutes* here employed is that of John Allen (1813), as revised and corrected by Benjamin B. Warfield, D.D., LL.D., and published by the Westminster Press, Philadelphia, Pa. (7th American edition). The selection from the *Commentaries on Romans* is in the translation by John Owen (1849). The passages from the *Commentaries on Daniel* are in the translation by Thomas Myers (1852). In both cases the selections reprinted here follow the texts of the complete editions published by Wm. B. Eerdmans Publishing Co., Grand Rapids, Mich.

Spelling and punctuation have been revised throughout to conform to current American usage. Editor's notes are indicated by brackets. In the following, references to the Church Fathers in the "Dedication" of the *Institutes* have been amplified for clarification. The number preceding the title corresponds to the number of the footnote in the "Dedication."

REFERENCES TO CHURCH FATHERS IN "DEDICATION"

(14) Augustinus, *In Joannis Evangelium*, tract. xiii, 14.

(23) Acacius of Amida, in Cassiodorus, *Historia tripartita*, XI, xvi; Ambrosius, *De Officiis ministrorum*, ii, 38.

(24) Spiridion, in Cassiodorus, *Historia tripartita*, I, x.

(25) Serapion, in Cassiodorus, *Historia tripartita*, VIII, i; Augustinus, *De Opere monachorum*, xvii, xxiii.

(26) Epiphanius, in Hieronymus, *Epistolae*, 51; Council of Elvira, canon 36.

(27) Ambrosius, *De Abraham*, I, vii.

(28) Pope Gelasius, *De duabus naturis Christi*. Cf. Darwell Stone, *History of the Doctrine of the Holy Eucharist* (London, 1905) I, 102.

(29) Chrysostomus, *Homiliae in Epistolam ad Ephesios*, iii, 5; (Pseudo) Calixtus, in Gratianus, *Decretum*, Pars III, Distinctio ii, Canon 10.

(30) Pope Gelasius, in Gratianus, *Decretum*, Pars III, Distinctio ii, Canon 12; Cyprianus, *Epistolae*, 63: 2:8; *De Lapsis*, 25.

(31) Augustinus, *De Peccatorum meritis et remissione*, II, xxxvi.

(32) Apollonius, in Eusebius, *Historia ecclesiastica*, V. xviii.

(33) Paphnutius, in Cassiodorus, *Historia tripartita*, II, xiv.

(34) Augustinus, *Contra Cresconium Grammaticum*, II, xxi.

(35) Cyprianus, *Epistolae*, 63:14.

(39) Hilarius Pictaviensis, *Contra Arianos vel Auxentium Mediolanensium*.

Selections from

INSTITUTES OF THE CHRISTIAN RELIGION

and

COMMENTARIES ON THE ROMANS AND ON DANIEL

To His Most Christian Majesty, Francis,
King of the French and his Sovereign,
John Calvin wisheth peace
and salvation in Christ

WHEN I BEGAN THIS WORK, Sire, nothing was further from my thoughts than writing a book which would afterwards be presented to your Majesty. My intention was only to lay down some elementary principles by which inquirers on the subject of religion might be instructed in the nature of true piety. And this labor I undertook chiefly for my countrymen, the French, of whom I apprehended multitudes to be hungering and thirsting after Christ, but saw very few possessing any real knowledge of him. That this was my design, the book itself proves by its simple method and unadorned composition. But when I perceived that the fury of certain wicked men in your kingdom had grown to such a height as to leave no room in the land for sound doctrine, I thought I should be usefully employed if in the same work I delivered my instructions to them, and exhibited my confession to you, that you may know the nature of that doctrine which is the object of such unbounded rage to those madmen who are now disturbing the country with fire and sword. For I shall not be afraid to acknowledge that this treatise contains a summary of that very doctrine which, according to their clamors, deserves to be punished with imprisonment, banishment, proscription, and flames, and to be exterminated from the face of the earth. I well know with what atrocious insinuations your ears have been filled by them in order to render our cause most odious in your esteem; but your clemency should lead you to consider that, if accusation be accounted a sufficient evidence of guilt, there will be an end of all innocence in words and actions. If anyone, indeed, with a view to bring an odium upon the doctrine which I am endeavoring to defend, should allege that it has long ago been

3

condemned by the general consent, and suppressed by many judicial decisions, this will be only equivalent to saying that it has been sometimes violently rejected through the influence and power of its adversaries, and sometimes insidiously and fraudulently oppressed by falsehoods, artifices, and calumnies. Violence is displayed when sanguinary sentences are passed against it without the cause being heard; and fraud, when it is unjustly accused of sedition and mischief. Lest anyone should suppose that these our complaints are unfounded, you yourself, Sire, can bear witness of the false calumnies with which you hear it daily traduced; that its only tendency is to wrest the scepters of kings out of their hands, to overturn all the tribunals and judicial proceedings, to subvert all order and governments, to disturb the peace and tranquility of the people, to abrogate all laws, to scatter all properties and possessions, and, in a word, to involve everything in total confusion. And yet you hear the smallest portion of what is alleged against it; for such horrible things are circulated among the vulgar that, if they were true, the whole world would justly pronounce it and its abettors worthy of a thousand fires and gibbets. Who, then, will wonder at its becoming the object of public odium, where credit is given to such most iniquitous accusations? This is the cause of the general consent and conspiracy to condemn us and our doctrine. Hurried away with this impulse, those who sit in judgment pronounce for sentences the prejudices they brought from home with them, and think their duty fully discharged if they condemn none to be punished but such as are convicted by their own confession or by sufficient proofs. Convicted of what crime? Of this condemned doctrine, they say. But with what justice is it condemned? Now, the ground of defense was not to abjure the doctrine itself, but to maintain its truth. On this subject, however, not a word is allowed to be uttered.

Wherefore I beseech you, Sire—and surely it is not an unreasonable request—to take upon yourself the entire cognizance of this cause which has hitherto been confusedly and carelessly agitated, without any order of law, and with outrageous passion rather than judicial gravity. Think not that I am now meditating my own individual defense in order to effect a safe return to my native country; for, though I feel the affection which every man ought to feel for it, yet, under the existing circumstances, I regret not my removal from it. But I plead the cause of all the godly, and consequently of Christ himself, which, having been in these times persecuted and trampled on in all ways in your kingdom, now lies in a most deplorable state; and this, indeed, rather through the tyranny of certain Pharisees than with your knowledge. How this comes to pass is foreign to my present purpose to say, but it certainly lies in a most afflicted state. For the ungodly have gone to such lengths that the truth of Christ, if not vanquished, dissipated, and entirely destroyed, is buried, as it were, in ignoble obscurity, while the poor, despised church is either destroyed by cruel massacres or driven away into banishment, or menaced and terrified into total silence. And still they continue their wonted madness and ferocity, pushing violently against the wall already bent, and finishing the ruin they have begun. In the meantime, no one comes forward to plead the cause against such furies. If there be any persons desirous of appearing most favorable to the truth, they only venture an opinion that forgiveness should be extended to the error and imprudence of ignorant people. For this is the language of these moderate men calling *that* error and imprudence which they know to be the certain truth of God, and *those* ignorant people whose understanding they perceive not to have been so despicable to Christ, but that he has favored them with the mysteries of his heavenly wisdom. Thus all are ashamed of the Gospel. But it shall be yours, Sire, not to turn away your ears or thoughts from so just a defense, especially in a cause of such importance as the maintenance of God's glory unimpaired in the world, the preservation of the honor of divine truth, and the continuance of the kingdom of Christ uninjured among us. This is a cause worthy of your attention, worthy of your cognizance, worthy of your throne. This consideration constitutes true royalty, to acknowledge yourself in the government of your kingdom to be the minister of God. For where the glory of God is not made the end of the government, it is not a legitimate sovereignty, but a usurpation. And he is deceived who expects lasting prosperity in that kingdom which is not ruled by the scepter of God, that is, his holy word; for that heavenly oracle cannot fail which declares that "where there is no vision, the people perish." [1] Nor should you be seduced from this pursuit by a contempt of our meanness. We are fully conscious to ourselves how very mean and abject we are, being miserable sinners before God, and accounted most despicable by men; being (if you please) the refuse of the world, deserving of the vilest appellations that can be found; so that nothing remains for us to glory in before God but his mercy alone, by which, without any merit of ours, we have been admitted to the hope of eternal salvation, and before men nothing but our weakness, the slightest confession of which is esteemed by them as the greatest disgrace. But our doctrine must stand, exalted above all the glory, and invincible by all the power of the world; because it is not ours but the doctrine of the living God, and of his Christ, whom the Father hath constituted King, that he may have dominion from sea to sea, and from the river even to the ends of the earth, and that he may rule in such a manner that the whole earth, with its strength of iron and with its splendor of gold and silver smitten by the rod of his mouth, may be broken to pieces like a potter's vessel; [2] for thus do the prophets foretell the magnificence of his kingdom.

Our adversaries reply that our pleading the word of God is a false pretense, and that we are nefarious corruptors of it. But that this is not only a malicious calumny but egregious impudence—by reading our confession, you will, in your wisdom, be able to judge. Yet something further is necessary to be said, to excite your attention or at least to prepare your mind for this perusal. Paul's direction that every prophecy

[1] Prov. 29:18.   [2] Dan. 2:34. Isaiah 11:4. Psalm 2:9.

be framed "according to the analogy of faith," [3] has fixed an invariable standard by which all interpretation of Scripture ought to be tried. If our principles be examined by this rule of faith, the victory is ours. For what is more consistent with faith than to acknowledge ourselves naked of all virtue, that we may be clothed by God; empty of all good, that we may be filled by him; slaves to sin, that we may be liberated by him; blind, that we may be enlightened by him; lame, that we may be guided; weak, that we may be supported by him; to divest ourselves of all ground of glorying, that he alone may be eminently glorious, and that we may glory in him? When we advance these and similar sentiments, they interrupt us with complaints that this is the way to overturn I know not what blind light of nature, pretended preparations, free will, and works meritorious of eternal salvation, together with all their supererogations; because they cannot bear that the praise and glory of all goodness, strength, righteousness, and wisdom should remain entirely with God. But we read of none being reproved for having drawn too freely from the fountain of living waters; on the contrary, they are severely upbraided who have "hewed them out cisterns, broken cisterns, that can hold no water." [4] Again, what is more consistent with faith than to assure ourselves of God being a propitious Father, where Christ is acknowledged as a Brother and Mediator, than securely to expect all prosperity and happiness from Him, whose unspeakable love toward us went so far that "he spared not his own Son, but delivered him up for us"; [5] than to rest in the certain expectation of salvation and eternal life, when we reflect upon the Father's gift of Christ, in whom such treasures are hidden? Here they oppose us and complain that this certainty of confidence is chargeable with arrogance and presumption. But as we ought to presume nothing of ourselves, so we should presume everything of God; nor are we divested of vain glory for any other reason than that we may learn to glory in the Lord. What shall I say more? Review, Sire, all the parts of our cause and

[3] Rom. 12:6.   [4] Jer. 2:13.   [5] Rom. 8:32.

consider us worse than the most abandoned of mankind unless you clearly discover that we thus "both labor and suffer reproach because we trust in the living God," [6] because
we believe that "this is life eternal to know the only true
God and Jesus Christ, whom he hath sent." [7] For this hope
some of us are bound in chains, others are lashed with
scourges, others are carried about as laughingstocks, others
are outlawed, others are cruelly tortured, others escape by
flight; but we are all reduced to extreme perplexities, exe-
crated with dreadful curses, cruelly slandered and treated
with the greatest indignities. Now, look at our adversaries (I
speak of the order of priests, at whose will and directions
others carry on these hostilities against us) and consider a
little with me by what principles they are actuated. The true
religion, which is taught in the Scriptures, and ought to be
universally maintained, they readily permit both themselves and others to be ignorant of, and to treat with neglect
and contempt. They think it unimportant what anyone holds
or denies concerning God and Christ provided he submits
his mind with an implicit faith (as they call it) to the judgment of the Church. Nor are they much affected if the glory
of God happens to be violated with open blasphemies, provided no one lift a finger against the primacy of the Apostolic
See and the authority of their holy Mother Church. Why,
therefore, do they contend with such extreme bitterness and
cruelty for the mass, purgatory, pilgrimages, and similar
trifles, and deny that any piety can be maintained without
a most explicit faith, so to speak, in these things; whereas
they prove none of them from the word of God? Why, but
because their belly is their god, their kitchen is their religion;
deprived of which they consider themselves no longer as
Christians or even as men. For though some feast themselves
in splendor, and others subsist on slender fare, yet all live on
the same pot, which, without this fuel, would not only cool
but completely freeze. Every one of them, therefore, who is
most solicitous for his belly, is found to be a most strenuous

6 I Tim. 4:10.   7 John 27:3.

champion for their faith. Indeed, they universally exert themselves for the preservation of their kingdom and the repletion
of their bellies, but not one of them discovers the least in-
dication of sincere zeal.

Nor do their attacks on our doctrine cease here; they urge
every topic of accusation and abuse to render it an object of
hatred or suspicion. They call it novel and of recent origin—
they cavil at it as doubtful and uncertain—they inquire by
what miracles it is confirmed—they ask whether it is right for
it to be received contrary to the consent of so many holy
fathers and the custom of the highest antiquity—they urge
us to confess that it is schismatical in stirring up opposition
against the Church, or that the Church was wholly extinct
for many ages during which no such thing was known—lastly,
they say all arguments are unnecessary; for that its nature
may be determined by its fruits, since it has produced such
a multitude of sects, so many factious tumults, and such great
licentiousness of vices. It is indeed very easy for them to insult a deserted cause with the credulous and ignorant multitude; but, if we had also the liberty of speaking in our turn,
this acrimony which they now discover in violently foaming
against us with equal licentiousness and impunity would
presently cool.

In the first place, their calling it novel is highly injurious
to God, whose holy word deserves not to be accused of novelty. I have no doubt of its being new to them to whom Jesus
Christ and the Gospel are equally new. But those who know
the antiquity of this preaching of Paul, "that Jesus Christ
died for our sins, and rose again for our justification," [8] will
find no novelty among us. That it has long been concealed,
buried, and unknown, is the crime of human impiety. Now
that the goodness of God has restored it to us, it ought at
least to be allowed its just claim of antiquity.

From the same source of ignorance springs the notion of
its being doubtful and uncertain. This is the very thing
which the Lord complains of by his prophet, that "the ox

[8] Rom. 4:25. I Cor. 25:3, 17.

knoweth his owner, and the ass his master's crib," [9] but that his people know not him. But however they may laugh at its uncertainty, if they were called to seal their own doctrine with their blood and lives, it would appear how much they value it. Very different is our confidence, which dreads neither the terrors of death nor even the tribunal of God.

Their requiring miracles of us is altogether unreasonable, for we forge no new Gospel but retain the very same whose truth was confirmed by all the miracles ever wrought by Christ and the apostles. But they have this peculiar advantage above us that they can confirm their faith by continual miracles even to this day. But the truth is, they allege miracles which are calculated to unsettle a mind otherwise well established; they are so frivolous and ridiculous, or vain and false. Nor, if they were ever so preternatural, ought they to have any weight in opposition to the truth of God, since the name of God ought to be sanctified in all places and at all times, whether by miraculous events or by the common order of nature. This fallacy might perhaps be more specious if the Scripture did not apprise us of the legitimate end and use of miracles. For Mark informs us that the miracles which followed the preaching of the apostles were wrought in confirmation [10] of it, and Luke tells us that [11] "the Lord gave testimony to the word of his grace," when "signs and wonders" were "done by the hands" of the apostles. Very similar to which is the assertion of the apostle that "salvation was confirmed" by the preaching of the Gospel: "God also bearing witness with signs and wonders and diverse miracles." [12] But those things which we are told were seals of the Gospel, shall we pervert to undermine the faith of the Gospel? Those things which were designed to be testimonials of the truth, shall we accommodate to the confirmation of falsehood? It is right, therefore, that the doctrine which, according to the evangelist, claims the first attention be examined and tried in the first place; and if it be approved, then it ought to derive confirmation from miracles. But it is the characteristic

[9] Isaiah 1:3.   [10] Mark 26:20.   [11] Acts 14:3.   [12] Heb. 2:3-4.

of sound doctrine, given by Christ, that it tends to promote, not the glory of men, but the glory of God.[13] Christ having laid down this proof of a doctrine, it is wrong to esteem those as miracles which are directed to any other end than the glorification of the name of God alone. And we should remember that Satan has his wonders which, though they are juggling tricks rather than real miracles, are such as to delude the ignorant and inexperienced. Magicians and enchanters have always been famous for miracles; idolatry has been supported by astonishing miracles; and yet we admit them not as proofs of the superstition of magicians or idolaters. With this engine also the simplicity of the vulgar was anciently assailed by the Donatists, who abounded in miracles. We therefore give the same answer now to our adversaries as Augustine [14] gave to the Donatists, that our Lord has cautioned us against these miraclemongers by his prediction that there should arise false prophets who, by various signs and lying wonders, "should deceive (if possible) the very elect." [15] And Paul has told us that the kingdom of Antichrist would be "with all power, and signs, and lying wonders." [16] But these miracles (they say) are wrought, not by idols or sorcerers, or false prophets, but by saints, as if we were ignorant that it is a stratagem of Satan to "transform" himself "into an angel of light." [17] At the tomb of Jeremiah,[18] who was buried in Egypt, the Egyptians formerly offered sacrifices and other divine honors. Was not this abusing God's holy prophet to the purposes of idolatry? Yet they supposed this veneration of his sepulchre to be rewarded with a cure for the bite of serpents. What shall we say but that it has been, and ever will be, the most righteous vengeance of God to "send those who receive not the love of the truth strong delusions, that they should believe a lie"? [19] We are by no means without miracles, and such as are cer-

13 John 7:18. 8:50.   14 [For complete reference see p. xxvi.]
15 Matt. 24:24.   16 II Thess. 2:9.   17 II Cor. 11:14.
18 *Cf.* C. C. Torrey, *The Lives of the Prophets,* Phil. (1946), pp. 21, 35.
19 II Thess. 2:10-11.

tain and not liable to cavils. But those under which they shelter themselves are mere illusions of Satan, seducing the people from the true worship of God to vanity.

Another calumny is their charging us with opposition to the fathers—I mean the writers of the earlier and purer ages—as if those writers were abettors of their impiety; whereas, if the contest were to be terminated by this authority, the victory in most parts of the controversy—to speak in the most modern terms—would be on our side. But though the writings of those fathers contain many wise and excellent things, yet in some respects they have suffered the common fate of mankind; these very dutiful children reverence only their errors and mistakes, but their excellences they either overlook or conceal or corrupt, so that it may be truly said to be their only study to collect dross from the midst of gold. Then they overwhelm us with senseless clamors, as despisers and enemies of the fathers. But we do not hold them in such contempt, but that, if it were consistent with my present design, I could easily support by their suffrages most of the sentiments that we now maintain. But while we make use of their writings, we always remember that "all things are ours," to serve us, not to have dominion over us, and that "we are Christ's" [20] alone, and owe him universal obedience. He who neglects this distinction will have nothing decided in religion, since those holy men were ignorant of many things, frequently at variance with each other, and sometimes even inconsistent with themselves. There is great reason, they say, for the admonition of Solomon "not to transgress or remove the ancient landmarks which our fathers have set." [21] But the same rule is not applicable to the bounding of fields and to the obedience of faith which ought to be ready to "forget her own people and her father's house." [22] But if they are so fond of allegorizing, why do they not explain the apostles, rather than any others, to be those fathers whose appointed landmarks it is so unlawful to remove? For this is the interpretation of Jerome, whose works they have received into

[20] I Cor. 3:21-23.   [21] Prov. 22:28.   [22] Psalm 45:10.

their canons. But if they insist on preserving the landmarks
of those whom they understand to be intended, why do they
at pleasure so freely transgress them themselves? There were
two fathers,[23] of whom one said that our God neither eats
nor drinks, and therefore needs neither cups nor dishes; the
other, that sacred things require no gold, and that gold is
no recommendation of that which is not purchased with
gold. This landmark therefore is transgressed by those who
in sacred things are so much delighted with gold, silver, ivory,
marble, jewels, and silks, and suppose that God is not rightly
worshipped unless all things abound in exquisite splendor,
or rather extravagant profusion. There was a father [24] who
said he freely partook of flesh on a day when others abstained
from it, because he was a Christian. They transgress the landmarks therefore when they curse the soul that tastes flesh in
Lent. There were two fathers,[25] of whom one said that a
monk who labors not with his hands is on a level with a
cheat or a robber; and the other, that it is unlawful for
monks to live on what is not their own, notwithstanding
their assiduity in contemplations, studies, and prayers; and
they have transgressed this landmark by placing the idle and
distended carcasses of monks in cells and brothels to be pam-
pered on the substances of others. There was a father [26] who
said that to see a painted image of Christ or of any saint, in
the temples of Christians, is a dreadful abomination. Nor
was this merely the sentence of an individual; it was also
decreed by an ecclesiastical council that the object of worship should not be painted on the walls. They are far from
confining themselves within these landmarks, for every corner
is filled with images. Another father [27] has advised that, after
having discharged the office of humanity toward the dead
by the rites of sepulture, we should leave them to their repose. They break through these landmarks by inculcating a
constant solicitude for the dead. There was one of the

23 Acacius of Amida [for complete reference see p. xxvi].

24 Spiridion [for complete reference see p. xxvi].

25 Serapion [see p. xxvi].   26 Epiphanius [see p. xxvi].

27 Ambrosius [see p. xxvi].

fathers [28] who asserted that the substance of bread and wine in the eucharist ceases not but remains, just as the substance of the human nature remains in the Lord Christ united with the divine. They transgress this landmark therefore by pretending that, on the words of the Lord being recited, the substance of bread and wine ceases and is transubstantiated into his body and blood. There were fathers [29] who, while they exhibited to the universal Church only one eucharist and forbade all scandalous and immoral persons to approach it, at the same time severely censured all who, when present, did not partake of it. How far have they removed these landmarks, when they fill not only the churches but even private houses with their masses, admit all who choose to be spectators of them, and everyone the more readily in proportion to the magnitude of his contribution, however chargeable with impurity and wickedness! They invite none to faith in Christ and a faithful participation of the sacraments, but rather for purposes of gain bring forward their own work instead of the grace and merit of Christ. There were two fathers [30] of whom one contended that the use of Christ's sacred supper should be wholly forbidden to those who, content with partaking of one kind, abstained from the other; the other strenuously maintained that Christian people ought not to be refused the blood of their Lord, for the confession of whom they are required to shed their own. These landmarks also they have removed in appointing, by an inviolable law, that very thing which the former punished with excommunication and the latter gave a powerful reason for disapproving. There was a father [31] who asserted the temerity of deciding on either side of an obscure subject, without clear and evident testimonies of Scripture. This landmark they forgot when they made so many constitutions, canons, and judicial determinations without any authority from the word of God. There was a father [32] who upbraided Montanus with

[28] Pope Gelasius [see p. xxvi].
[29] Chrysostomus [see p. xxvi].
[30] Pope Gelasius [see p. xxvi].
[31] Augustinus [see p. xxvi].
[32] Apollonius [see p. xxvi].

having, among other heresies, been the first imposer of laws for the observance of fasts. They have gone far beyond this landmark also, in establishing fasts by the strictest laws. There was a father [33] who denied that marriage ought to be forbidden to the ministers of the Church, and pronounced cohabitation with a wife to be real chastity; and there were fathers who assented to his judgment. They have transgressed these landmarks by enjoining on their priests the strictest celibacy. There was a father who thought that attention should be paid to Christ only, of whom it is said, "Hear ye him," and that no regard should be had to what others before us have either said or done, only to what has been commanded by Christ, who is pre-eminent over all. This landmark they neither prescribe to themselves, nor permit to be observed by others, when they set up over themselves and others any masters rather than Christ. There was a father [34] who contended that the Church ought not take the precedence of Christ because his judgment is always according to truth, but ecclesiastical judges, like other men, may generally be deceived. Breaking down this landmark also, they scruple not to assert that all the authority of the Scripture depends on the decision of the Church. All the fathers, with one heart and voice, have declared it execrable and detestable for the holy word of God to be contaminated with the subtleties of sophists and perplexed by the wrangles of logicians. Do they confine themselves within these landmarks when the whole business of their lives is to involve the simplicity of the Scripture in endless controversies, and worse than sophistical wrangles, so that if the fathers were now restored to life and heard this art of wrangling, which they call speculative divinity, they would not suspect the dispute to have the least reference to God. But if I would enumerate all the instances in which the authority of the fathers is insolently rejected by those who would be thought their dutiful children, my address would exceed all reasonable bounds. Months

33 Paphnutius [see p. xxvi].
34 Augustinus [for complete reference see p. xxvi].

and years would be insufficient for me. And yet such is their consummate and incorrigible impudence, they dare to censure us for presuming to transgress the ancient landmarks.

Nor can they gain any advantage against us by their argument from custom; for, if we were compelled to submit to custom, we should have to complain of the greatest injustice. Indeed, if the judgments of men were correct, custom should be sought among the good. But the fact is often very different. What appears to be practiced by many soon obtains the force of a custom. And human affairs have scarcely ever been in so good a state as for the majority to be pleased with things of real excellence. From the private vices of multitudes, therefore, has arisen public error, or rather a common agreement of vices, which these good men would now have to be received as law. It is evident to all who can see that the world is inundated with more than an ocean of evils, that it is overrun with numerous destructive pests, that everything is fast verging to ruin, so that we must altogether despair of human affairs or vigorously and even violently oppose such immense evils. And the remedy is rejected for no other reason but because we have been accustomed to the evils so long. But let public error be tolerated in human society; in the kingdom of God nothing but his eternal truth should be heard and regarded, which no succession of years, no custom, no confederacy can circumscribe. Thus Isaiah once taught the chosen people of God: "Say ye not, A confederacy, to all to whom this people shall say, A confederacy"; that is, that they should not unite in the wicked consent of the people; "nor fear their fear, nor be afraid," but rather "sanctify the Lord of hosts," that he might "be their fear and their dread." [35] Now, therefore, let them, if they please, object against us past ages and present examples; if we "sanctify the Lord of hosts," we shall not be much afraid. For, whether many ages agree in similar impiety, he is mighty to take vengeance on the third and fourth generation; or whether the whole world combine in the same iniquity, he

[35] Isaiah 8:12-13.

has given an example of the fatal end of those who sin with
a multitude, by destroying all men with a deluge, and preserving Noah and his small family in order that his individual faith might condemn the whole world. Lastly, a corrupt custom is nothing but an epidemical pestilence, which
is equally fatal to its objects, though they fall with a multitude. Besides, they ought to consider a remark, somewhere
made by Cyprian,[36] that persons who sin through ignorance,
though they cannot be wholly exculpated, may yet be considered in some degree excusable; but those who obstinately
reject the truth offered by the Divine goodness are without
any excuse at all.

Nor are we so embarrassed by their dilemma as to be
obliged to confess either that the Church was for some time
extinct or that we have now a controversy with the Church.
The Church of Christ has lived and will continue to live as
long as Christ shall reign at the right hand of the Father,
by whose hand she is sustained, by whose protection she is
defended, by whose power she is preserved in safety. For he
will undoubtedly perform what he once promised, to be with
his people "even to the end of the word." [37] We have no
quarrel against the Church, for with one consent we unite
with all the company of the faithful in worshipping and
adoring the one God and Christ the Lord, as he has been
adored by all the pious in all ages. But our opponents deviate widely from the truth when they acknowledge no Church
but what is visible to the corporeal eye, and endeavor to circumscribe it by those limits within which it is far from being
included. Our controversy turns on the two following points:
first, they contend that the form of the Church is always
apparent and visible; secondly, they place that form in the
see of the Roman Church and her order of prelates. We assert, on the contrary, first, that the Church may exist without
any visible form; secondly, that its form is not contained in
that external splendor which they foolishly admire, but is
distinguished by a very different criterion, namely, the pure

[36] [For complete reference see p. xxvi].   [37] Matt. 28:20.

preaching of God's word, and the legitimate administration
of the sacraments. They are not satisfied unless the Church
can always be pointed out with the finger. But how often
among the Jewish people was it so disorganized as to have
no visible form left? What splendid form do we suppose
could be seen, when Elias deplored his being left alone? [38]
How long, after the coming of Christ, did it remain without
any external form? How often, since that time, have wars,
seditions, and heresies oppressed and totally obscured it? If
they had lived at that period, would they have believed that
any Church existed? Yet Elias was informed that there were
"left seven thousand" who had "not bowed the knee to Baal."
Nor should we entertain any doubt of Christ's having always
reigned on earth ever since his ascension to heaven. But if
the pious at such periods had sought for any form evident
to their senses, must not their hearts have been quite dis-
couraged? Indeed, it was already considered by Hilary in his
day as a grievous error that people were absorbed in foolish
admiration of the episcopal dignity and did not perceive the
dreadful mischiefs concealed under that disguise. For this is
his language: [39]

One thing I advise you—beware of Antichrist, for you have
an improper attachment to walls; your veneration for the
Church of God is misplaced on houses and buildings; you
wrongly introduce under them the name of peace. Is there
any doubt that they will be seats of Antichrist? I think moun-
tains, woods, and lakes, prisons, and whirlpools less dangerous; for these were the scenes of retirement or banishment in
which the prophets prophesied.

But what excites the veneration of the multitude in the present day for their horned bishops but the supposition that
those are the holy prelates of religion whom they see presiding over great cities? Away, then, with such stupid admiration. Let us rather leave it to the Lord, since he alone "know-

[38] I Kings 19:14, 18.
[39] Hilarius Pictaviensis [for complete reference see p. xxvi].

eth them that are his," [40] sometimes to remove from human observation all external knowledge of his Church. I admit this to be a dreadful judgment of God on the earth; but if it be deserved by the impiety of men, why do we attempt to resist the righteous vengeance of God? Thus the Lord punished the ingratitude of men in former ages; for, in consequence of their resistance to his truth, and extinction of the light he had given them, he permitted them to be blinded by sense, deluded by absurd falsehoods, and immerged in profound darkness, so that there was no appearance of the true Church left; yet, at the same time, in the midst of darkness and errors, he preserved his scattered and concealed people from total destruction. Nor is this to be wondered at, for he knew how to save in all the confusion of Babylon, and the flame of the fiery furnace. But how dangerous it is to estimate the form of the Church by I know not what vain pomp, which they contend for, I shall rather briefly suggest than state at large, lest I should protract this discourse to an excessive length. The Pope, they say, who holds the Apostolic see, and the bishops anointed and consecrated by him, provided they are equipped with miters and crosiers, represent the Church and ought to be considered as the Church. Therefore they cannot err. How is this?—Because they are pastors of the Church, and consecrated to the Lord. And did not the pastoral character belong to Aaron and the other rulers of Israel? Yet Aaron and his sons, after their designation to the priesthood, fell into error when they made the golden calf.[41] According to this mode of reasoning, why should not the four hundred prophets, who lied to Ahab, have represented the Church? [42] But the Church remained on the side of Micaiah, solitary and despised as he was, and out of his mouth proceeded the truth. Did not those prophets exhibit both the name and appearance of the Church, who with united violence rose up against Jeremiah, and threatened and boasted, "the law shall not perish from the priest, nor

40 II Tim. 2:19.   41 Exod. 32:4.   42 I Kings 22:6, 11-23.

counsel from the wise, nor the word from the prophet?" [43]
Jeremiah is sent singly against the whole multitude of
prophets, with a denunciation from the Lord, that the "law
shall perish from the priest, counsel from the wise, and the
word from the prophet." [44] And was there not the like external respectability in the council convened by the chief
priests, scribes, and Pharisees, to consult about putting Christ
to death? [45] Now, let them go and adhere to the external
appearance, and thereby make Christ and all the prophets
schismatics, and, on the other hand, make the ministers of
Satan instruments of the Holy Spirit. But if they speak their
real sentiments, let them answer me sincerely what nation
or place they consider as the seat of the Church, from the
time when, by a decree of the Council of Basel, Eugenius was
deposed and degraded from the pontificate, and Amadeus
substituted in his place. They cannot deny that the council,
as far as relates to external forms, was a lawful one, and summoned not only by one pope but by two. There Eugenius
was pronounced guilty of schism, rebellion, and obstinacy,
together with all the host of cardinals and bishops who had
joined him in attempting a dissolution of the council. Yet
afterwards, assisted by the favor of princes, he regained the
quiet possession of his former dignity. That election of
Amadeus, though formally made by the authority of a general and holy synod, vanished into smoke; and he was ap-
peased with a cardinal's hat, like a barking dog with a morsel.
From the bosom of those heretics and rebels have proceeded
all the popes, cardinals, bishops, abbots, and priests ever
since. Here they must stop. For to which party will they give
the title of the Church? Will they deny that this was a general council which wanted nothing to complete its external
majesty, being solemnly convened by two papal bulls, consecrated by a presiding legate of the Roman see, and well
regulated in every point of order, and invariably preserving
the same dignity to the last? Will they acknowledge Eugenius
to be a schismatic, with all his adherents, by whom they have

[43] Jer. 18:18.   [44] Jer. 4:9.   [45] Matt. 26:3-4.

all been consecrated? Either, therefore, let them give a different definition of the form of the Church or, whatever be their number, we shall account them all schismatics, as having been knowingly and voluntarily ordained by heretics. But if it had never been ascertained before that the Church is not confined to external pomps, they would themselves afford us abundant proof of it who have so long superciliously exhibited themselves to the world under the title of the Church, though they were at the same time the deadly plagues of it. I speak not of their morals and those tragical exploits with which all their lives abound, since they profess themselves to be Pharisees, who are to be heard and not imitated. I refer to the very doctrine itself on which they found their claim to be considered as the Church. If you devote a portion of your leisure, Sire, to the perusal of our writings, you will clearly discover that doctrine to be a fatal pestilence of souls, the firebrand, ruin, and destruction of the Church.

Finally, they betray great want of candor by invidiously repeating what great commotions, tumults, and contentions have attended the preaching of our doctrine, and what effects it produces in many persons. For it is unfair to charge it with those evils which ought to be attributed to the malice of Satan. It is the native property of the Divine word never to make its appearance without disturbing Satan and rousing his opposition. This is the most certain and unequivocal criterion by which it is distinguished from false doctrines, which are easily broached when they are heard with general attention and received with applauses by the world. Thus, in some ages, when all things were immerged in profound darkness, the prince of this world amused and diverted himself with the generality of mankind and, like another Sardanapalus, gave himself up to his ease and pleasures in perfect peace; for what would he do but amuse and divert himself in the quiet and undisturbed possession of his kingdom? But when the light shining from above dissipated a portion of his darkness—when that Mighty One alarmed and assaulted his kingdom—then he began to shake off his wonted torpor and to hurry on his armor. First, indeed, he stirred up the power of men to suppress the truth by violence at its first appearance; and when this proved ineffectual, he had recourse to subtlety. He made the Catabaptists, and other infamous characters, the instruments of exciting dissensions and doctrinal controversies, with a view to obscure and finally to extinguish it. And now he continues to attack it in both ways, for he endeavors to root up this genuine seed by means of human force, and at the same time tries every effort to choke it with his tares that it may not grow and produce fruit. But all his attempts will be vain if we attend to the admonitions of the Lord, who has long ago made us acquainted with his devices, that we might not be caught by him unawares, and has armed us with sufficient means of defense against all his assaults. But to charge the word of God with the odium of seditions, excited against it by wicked and rebellious men, or of sects raised by impostors—is not this extreme malignity? Yet it is not without example in former times. Elias was asked whether it was not he "that troubled Israel." [46] Christ was represented by the Jews as guilty of sedition.[47] The apostles were accused of stirring up popular commotions.[48] Wherein does this differ from the conduct of those who, at the present day, impute to us all the disturbances, tumults, and contentions that break out against us? But the proper answer to such accusations has been taught us by Elias —that the dissemination of errors and the raising of tumults is not chargeable on us, but on those who are resisting the power of God. But as this one reply is sufficient to repress their temerity, so, on the other hand, we must meet the weakness of some persons who are frequently disturbed with such offenses and become unsettled and wavering in their minds. Now, that they may not stumble and fall amidst this agitation and perplexity, let them know that the apostles in their day experienced the same things that now befall us. There were "unlearned and unstable" men, Peter says, who "wrested"

[46] I Kings 18:17.   [47] Luke 23:2, 5.   [48] Acts 17:6. 24:5.

the inspired writings of Paul "to their own destruction." [49]
There were despisers of God who, when they heard that
"where sin abounded grace did much more abound," immediately concluded, Let us "continue in sin, that grace may
abound." When they heard that the faithful were "not under
the law," they immediately croaked, "We will sin, because we
are not under the law, but under grace." [50] There were some
who accused him as an encourager of sin. Many false apostles
crept in to destroy the churches he had raised. "Some
preached" the gospel "of envy and strife, not in sincerity,"
maliciously "supposing to add affliction to his bonds." [51] In
some places the Gospel was attended with little benefit. "All
were seeking their own, not the things of Jesus Christ." [52]
Others returned "like dogs to their vomit, and like swine to
their wallowing in the mire." [53] Many perverted the liberty
of the spirit into the licentiousness of the flesh. Many in-
sinuated themselves as brethren, who afterwards brought the
pious into dangers. Various contentions were excited among
the brethren themselves. What was to be done by the apostles
in such circumstances? Should they not have dissembled for
a time, or rather have rejected and deserted that Gospel
which appeared to be the nursery of so many disputes, the
cause of so many dangers, the occasion of so many offenses?
But in such difficulties as these, their minds were relieved by
this reflection that Christ is the "stone of stumbling and rock
of offense," [54] "set for the fall and rising again of many, and
for a sign which shall be spoken against"; [55] and armed with
this confidence, they proceeded boldly through all the dangers of tumults and offenses. The same consideration should
support us, since Paul declares it to be the perpetual character of the Gospel, that it is "a savior of death unto death
in them that perish," [56] although it was rather given us to
be the "savior of life unto life," and "the power of God to"
the "salvation" of the faithful,[57] which we also should cer-

49 II Pet. 3:16.   50 Rom. 5:20. 6:1, 14-15.   51 Phil. 1:15-16.
52 Phil. 2:21.   53 Pet. 2:22.   54 I Pet. 2:8.
55 Luke 2:34.   56 II Cor. 2:15-16.   57 Rom. 1:16.

tainly experience it to be, if we did not corrupt this eminent
gift of God by our ingratitude, and pervert to our destruction
what ought to be a principal instrument of our salvation.

But I return to you, Sire. Let not your Majesty be at all
moved by those groundless accusations with which our adversaries endeavor to terrify you; as that the sole tendency
and design of this new Gospel—for so they call it—is to furnish a pretext for seditions and to gain impunity for all
crimes. "For God is not the author of confusion, but of
peace"; [58] nor is "the Son of God," who came to "destroy the
works of the devil, the minister of sin." [59] And it is unjust to
charge us with such motives and designs of which we have
never given cause for the least suspicion. Is it probable that
we are meditating the subversion of kingdoms?—We who were
never heard to utter a factious word, whose lives were ever
known to be peaceable and honest while we lived under your
government, and who, even now in our exile, cease not to
pray for all prosperity to attend yourself and your kingdom!
Is it probable that we are seeking an unlimited license to
commit crimes with impunity in whose conduct, though many
things may be blamed, yet there is nothing worthy of such
severe reproach? Nor have we, by divine grace, profited so
little in the Gospel but that our life may be an example to
our detractors of chastity, liberality, mercy, temperance, patience, modesty, and every other virtue. It is an undeniable
fact that we sincerely fear and worship God, whose name
we desire to be sanctified both by our life and by our death;
and envy itself is constrained to bear testimony to the innocence and civil integrity of some of us who have suffered the
punishment of death for that very thing which ought to be
accounted their highest praise. But if the Gospel be made a
pretext for tumults, which has not yet happened in your
kingdom; if any persons make the liberty of divine grace an
excuse for the licentiousness of their vices, of whom I have
known many—there are laws and legal penalties by which
they may be punished according to their deserts; only let not

[58] I Cor. 14:33.   [59] I John 3:8. Gal. 2:17.

the Gospel of God be reproached for the crimes of wicked men. You have now, Sire, the virulent iniquity of our calumniators laid before you in a sufficient number of instances, that you may not receive their accusations with too credulous an ear—I fear I have gone too much into the detail, as this preface already approaches the size of a full apology, whereas I intended it not to contain our defense, but only to prepare your mind to attend to the pleading of our cause; for, though you are now averse and alienated from us, and even inflamed against us, we despair not of regaining your favor, if you will only once read with calmness and composure this our confession, which we intend as our defense before your Majesty. But, on the contrary, if your ears are so preoccupied with the whispers of the malevolent as to leave no opportunity for the accused to speak for themselves, and if those outrageous furies, with your connivance, continue to persecute with imprisonments, scourges, tortures, confiscations, and flames, we shall indeed, like sheep destined to the slaughter, be reduced to the greatest extremities. Yet shall we in patience possess our souls and wait for the mighty hand of the Lord, which undoubtedly will in time appear and show itself armed for the deliverance of the poor from their affliction, and for the punishment of their despisers, who now exult in such perfect security. May the Lord, the King of kings, establish your throne with righteousness, and your kingdom with equity.

ON CHRISTIAN LIBERTY

WE HAVE NOW to treat of Christian liberty, an explanation of which ought not to be omitted in a treatise which is designed to comprehend a compendious summary of evangelical doctrine. For it is a subject of the first importance, and unless it be well understood, our consciences scarcely venture to undertake anything without doubting, experience in many things hesitation and reluctance, and are always subject to fluctuations and fears. But especially it is an appendix to justification and affords no small assistance toward the knowledge of its influence. Hence they who sincerely fear God will experience the incomparable advantage of that doctrine which impious scoffers pursue with their railleries; because in the spiritual intoxication with which they are seized, they allow themselves the most unbounded impudence. Wherefore this is the proper time to introduce the subject; and though we have slightly touched upon it on some former occasions, yet it was useful to defer the full discussion of it to this place; because, as soon as any mention is made of Christian liberty, then either inordinate passions rage or violent emotions arise unless timely opposition be made to those wanton spirits who most nefariously corrupt things which are otherwise the best. For some, under the pretext of this liberty, cast off all obedience to God and precipitate themselves into the most unbridled licentiousness; and some despise it, supposing it to be subversive of all moderation, order, and moral distinctions. What can we do in this case, surrounded by such difficulties? Shall we entirely discard Christian liberty and so preclude the occasion of such dangers? But, as we have observed, unless this be understood, there can be no right knowledge of Christ or of evangelical truth or of internal peace of mind. We should rather exert ourselves to prevent the suppression of such a necessary branch of doctrine, and at the same time to obviate those absurd objections which are frequently deduced from it.

II. Christian liberty, according to my judgment, consists of three parts. The first part is that the consciences of believers, when seeking an assurance of their justification before God, should raise themselves above the law and forget all the righteousness of the law. For since the law, as we have elsewhere demonstrated, leaves no man righteous, either we must be excluded from all hope of justification or it is necessary for us to be delivered from it, and that so completely as not to have any dependence on works. For he who imagines that in order to obtain righteousness he must produce any works, however small, can fix no limit or boundary, but renders himself a debtor to the whole law. Avoiding, therefore, all mention of the law and dismissing all thought of our own works, in reference to justification, we must embrace the Divine mercy alone, and turning our eyes from ourselves, fix them solely on Christ. For the question is not how we can be righteous, but how, though unrighteous and unworthy, we can be considered as righteous. And the conscience that desires to attain any certainty respecting this must give no admission to the law. Nor will this authorize anyone to conclude that the law is of no use to believers, whom it still continues to instruct and exhort and stimulate to duty, although it has no place in their consciences before the tribunal of God. For these two things, being very different, require to be properly and carefully distinguished by us. The whole life of Christians ought to be an exercise of piety, since they are called to sanctification.[1] It is the office of the law to remind them of their duty and thereby to excite them to the pursuit of holiness and integrity. But when their consciences are solicitous how God may be propitiated, what answer they shall make, and on what they shall rest their confidence, if called to his tribunal, there must then be no consideration of the requisitions of the law, but Christ alone must be proposed for righteousness, who exceeds all the perfection of the law.

III. On this point turns almost the whole argument of the Epistle to the Galatians. For that they are erroneous expositors

[1] Ephes. 1:4. I Thess. 4:3, 7.

who maintain that Paul there contends only for liberty from ceremonies may be proved from the topics of his reasoning, such as these: "Christ hath redeemed us from the curse of the law, being made a curse for us." [2] Again:

Stand fast, therefore, in the liberty, wherewith Christ hath made us free, and be not entangled again with the yoke of bondage. Behold, I Paul say unto you, that if ye be circumcised, Christ shall profit you nothing. Every man that is circumcised is a debtor to do the whole law; ye are fallen from grace.[3]

These passages certainly comprehend something more exalted than a freedom from ceremonies. I confess, indeed, that Paul is there treating of ceremonies, because he is contending with the false apostles who attempted to introduce again into the Christian Church the ancient shadows of the law, which had been abolished by the advent of Christ. But for the decision of this question it was necessary to discuss some higher topics in which the whole controversy lay. First, because the brightness of the Gospel was obscured by those Jewish shadows, he shows that in Christ we have a complete exhibition of all those things which were adumbrated by the ceremonies of Moses. Secondly, because these imposters instilled into the people the very pernicious opinion that this ceremonial obedience was sufficient to merit the Divine favor, he principally contends that believers ought not to suppose that they can obtain righteousness before God by any works of the law, much less by those inferior elements. And he at the same time teaches that from the condemnation of the law, which otherwise impends over all men, they are delivered by the Cross of Christ, that they may rely with perfect security on him alone—a topic which properly belongs to our present subject. Lastly, he asserts the liberty of the consciences of believers, which ought to be laid under no obligation in things that are not necessary.

IV. The second part of Christian liberty, which is dependent on the first, is that their consciences do not observe the law, as being under any legal obligation; but that, being lib-

2 Gal. 3:13   3 Gal. 5:1-4.

erated from the yoke of the law, they yield a voluntary obedience to the will of God. For being possessed with perpetual terrors, as long as they remain under the dominion of the law, they will never engage with alacrity and promptitude in the service of God unless they have previously received this liberty. We shall more easily and clearly discover the design of these things from an example. The precept of the law is, "Thou shalt love the Lord thy God with all thine heart, and with all thy soul, and with all thy might." [4] That this command may be fulfilled, our soul must be previously divested of every other perception and thought, our heart must be freed from all desires, and our might must be collected and contracted to this one point. Those who, compared with others, have made a very considerable progress in the way of the Lord, are yet at an immense distance from this perfection. For though they love God with their soul and with sincere affection of heart, yet they have still much of their heart and soul occupied by carnal desires, which retard their progress toward God. They do indeed press forward with strong exertions, but the flesh partly debilitates their strength, and partly attracts it to itself. What can they do in this case, when they perceive that they are so far from observing the law? They wish, they aspire, they endeavor, but they do nothing with the perfection that is required. If they advert to the law, they see that every work they attempt or meditate is accursed. Nor is there the least reason for any person to deceive himself by concluding that an action is not necessarily altogether evil because it is imperfect, and that therefore the good part of it is accepted by God. For the law, requiring perfect love, condemns all imperfection unless its rigor be mitigated. Let him consider his work, therefore, which he wished to be thought partly good, and he will find that very work to be a transgression of the law because it is imperfect.

V. See how all our works, if estimated according to the rigor of the law, are subject to its curse. How, then, could unhappy souls apply themselves with alacrity to any work for

[4] Deut. 6:5.

which they could expect to receive nothing but a curse? On the contrary, if they are liberated from the severe exaction of the law or rather from the whole of its rigor, and hear God calling them with paternal gentleness, then with cheerfulness and prompt alacrity they will answer to his call and follow his guidance. In short, they who are bound by the yoke of the law are like slaves who have certain daily tasks appointed by their masters. They think they have done nothing, and presume not to enter into the presence of their masters without having finished the work prescribed to them. But children who are treated by their parents in a more liberal manner hesitate not to present to them their imperfect and in some respects faulty works, in confidence that their obedience and promptitude of mind will be accepted by them, though they have not performed all that they wished. Such children ought we to be, feeling a certain confidence that our services, however small, rude, and imperfect, will be approved by our most indulgent Father. This he also confirms to us by the prophet: "I will spare them," saith he, "as a man spareth his own son that serveth him"; [5] where it is evident, from the mention of "service," that the word "spare" is used to denote indulgence, or an overlooking of faults. And we have great need of this confidence, without which all our endeavors will be vain; for God considers us as serving him in none of our works but such as are truly done by us to his honor. But how can this be done amidst those terrors, where it is a matter of doubt whether our works offend God or honor him?

VI. This is the reason why the author of the Epistle to the Hebrews refers to faith, and estimates only by faith, all the good works which are recorded of the holy patriarchs.[6] On this liberty there is a remarkable passage in the Epistle to the Romans, where Paul reasons that sin ought not to have dominion over us because we are not under the law, but under grace.[7] For after he had exhorted believers, "Let not sin, therefore, reign in your mortal body; neither yield ye your members as instruments of unrighteousness; but yield yourselves unto

[5] Mal. 3:17.   [6] Heb. 11:2.   [7] Rom. 6:14.

God, as those that are alive from the dead, and your members as instruments of righteousness unto God," [8] they might, on the contrary, object that they yet carried about with them the flesh full of inordinate desires, and that sin dwelt in them; but he adds the consolation furnished by their liberty from the law, as though he had said, Although you do not yet experience sin to be destroyed and righteousness living in you in perfection, yet you have no cause for terror and dejection of mind, as if God were perpetually offended on account of your remaining sin; because by grace you are emancipated from the law, that your works may not be judged according to that rule. But those who infer that we may commit sin because we are not under the law may be assured that they have no concern with this liberty the end of which is to animate us to virtue.

VII. The third part of Christian liberty teaches us that we are bound by no obligation before God respecting external things, which in themselves are indifferent, but that we may indifferently sometimes use and at other times omit them. And the knowledge of this liberty also is very necessary for us; for without it we shall have no tranquility of conscience, nor will there be any end of superstitions. Many in the present age think it a folly to raise any dispute concerning the free use of meats, of days, and of habits, and similar subjects, considering these things as frivolous and nugatory; but they are of greater importance than is generally believed. For when the conscience has once fallen into the snare, it enters a long and inextricable labyrinth from which it is afterwards difficult to escape; if a man begin to doubt the lawfulness of using flax in sheets, shirts, handkerchiefs, napkins, and tablecloths, neither will he be certain respecting hemp, and at last he will doubt of the lawfulness of using tow; for he will consider with himself whether he cannot eat without tablecloths or napkins, whether he cannot do without handkerchiefs. If anyone imagine delicate food to be unlawful, he will ere long have no tranquility before God in eating brown bread and

[8] Rom. 6:12-13.

common viands, while he remembers that he might support
his body with meat of a quality still inferior. If he hesitate
respecting good wine, he will afterwards be unable with any
peace of conscience to drink the most vapid; and at last he
will not presume even to touch purer and sweeter water than
others. In short, he will come to think it criminal to step
over a twig that lies across his path. For this is the commence-
ment of no trivial controversy; but the dispute is whether
the use of certain things be agreeable to God, whose will
ought to guide all our resolutions and all our actions. The
necessary consequence is that some are hurried by despair into
a vortex of confusion, from which they see no way of escape;
and some, despising God and casting off all fear of him, make
a way of ruin for themselves. For all who are involved in such
doubts, which way soever they turn their views, behold something offensive to their consciences presenting itself on every
side.

VIII. "I know," says Paul, "that there is nothing unclean
of itself; but to him that esteemeth anything to be unclean,
to him it is unclean." [9] In these words he makes all external
things subject to our liberty, provided that our minds have
regard to this liberty before God. But if any superstitious
notion cause us to scruple, those things which were naturally
pure become contaminated to us. Wherefore he subjoins,
"Happy is he that condemneth not himself in that which he
alloweth. And he that doubteth is condemned if he eat, because he eateth not of faith; for whatsoever is not of faith is
sin." [10] Are not they who in these perplexities show their superior boldness by the security of their presumption guilty of
departing from God, whilst they who are deeply affected with
the true fear of God, when they are even constrained to admit many things to which their own consciences are averse, are
filled with terror and consternation? No persons of this description receive any of the gifts of God with thanksgiving,
by which alone Paul, nevertheless, declares them to be all
sanctified to our use.[11] I mean a thanksgiving proceeding from

[9] Rom. 14:14.   [10] Rom. 14:22-23.   [11] I Tim. 4:5.

a mind which acknowledges the beneficence and goodness of God in the blessings he bestows. For many of them, indeed, apprehend the good things which they use to be from God, whom they praise in his works; but not being persuaded that they are given to them, how could they give thanks to God as the giver of them? We see, in short, the tendency of this liberty, which is that, without any scruple of conscience or perturbation of mind, we should devote the gifts of God to that use for which he has given them; by which confidence our souls may have peace with him and acknowledge his liberality toward us. For this comprehends all ceremonies, the observation of which is left free, that the conscience may not be bound by any obligation to observe them, but may remember that by the goodness of God it may use them or abstain from them, as shall be most conducive to edification.

IX. Now it must be carefully observed that Christian liberty is in all its branches a spiritual thing; all the virtue of which consists in appeasing terrified consciences before God, whether they are disquieted and solicitous concerning the remission of their sins or are anxious to know if their works, which are imperfect and contaminated by the defilements of the flesh, be acceptable to God; or are tormented concerning the use of things that are indifferent. Wherefore they are guilty of perverting its meaning who either make it the pretext of their irregular appetites, that they may abuse the Divine blessings to the purposes of sensuality, or who suppose that there is no liberty but what is used before men, and therefore in the exercise of it totally disregard their weak brethren. The former of these sins is the more common in the present age. There is scarcely anyone whom his wealth permits to be sumptuous, who is not delighted with luxurious splendor in his entertainments, in his dress, and in his buildings; who does not desire a pre-eminence in every species of luxury; who does not strangely flatter himself on his elegance. And all these things are defended under the pretext of Christian liberty. They allege that they are things indifferent; this I admit provided they be indifferently used. But where they are too ardently coveted, proudly boasted, or luxuriously lavished, these things, of themselves otherwise indifferent, are completely polluted by such vices. This passage of Paul makes an excellent distinction respecting things which are indifferent: "Unto the pure all things are pure; but unto them that are defiled and unbelieving is nothing pure; but even their mind and conscience are defiled." [12] For why are curses denounced on rich men, who "receive their consolation," who are "satiated," who "now laugh," who "lie on beds of ivory," who "join field to field," who "have the harp, and the lyre, and the tabret, and wine in their feasts"? [13] Ivory and gold, and riches of all kinds, are certainly blessings of Divine Providence, not only permitted, but expressly designed for the use of men; nor are we anywhere prohibited to laugh or to be satiated with food, or to annex new possessions to those already enjoyed by ourselves or by our ancestors, or to be delighted with musical harmony, or to drink wine. This indeed is true; but amidst an abundance of all things, to be immersed in sensual delights, to inebriate the heart and mind with present pleasures, and perpetually to grasp at new ones—these things are very remote from a legitimate use of the Divine blessings. Let them banish, therefore, immoderate cupidity, excessive profusion, vanity, and arrogance; that with a pure conscience they may make a proper use of the gifts of God. When their hearts shall be formed to this sobriety, they will have a rule for the legitimate enjoyment of them. On the contrary, without this moderation even common and ordinary pleasures are chargeable with excess. For it is truly observed that a proud heart frequently dwells under coarse and ragged garments, and that simplicity and humility are sometimes concealed under purple and fine linen. Let all men, in their respective stations, whether of poverty, of competence, or of splendor, live in the remembrance of this truth that God confers his blessings on them for the support of life, not for luxury; and let them consider this as the law of Christian liberty that they learn the lesson which Paul had learned, when

[12] Titus 1:15.   [13] Luke 6:24–25. Amos 6:1f. Isaiah 5:8f.

he said, "I have learned, in whatsoever state I am, therewith to be content. I know both how to be abased, and I know how to abound: everywhere and in all things I am instructed both to be full and to be hungry, both to abound and to suffer need." [14]

X. Many persons err likewise in this respect that, as if their liberty would not be perfectly secure unless witnessed by men, they make an indiscriminate and imprudent use of it—a disorderly practice which occasions frequent offense to their weak brethren. There are some to be found, in the present day, who imagine their liberty would be abridged if they were not to enter on the enjoyment of it by eating animal food on Friday. Their eating is not the subject of my reprehension; but their minds require to be divested of this false notion; for they ought to consider that they obtain no advantage from their liberty before men, but with God; and that it consists in abstinence as well as in use. If they apprehend it to be immaterial in God's view whether they eat animal food or eggs, whether their garments be scarlet or black, it is quite sufficient. The conscience to which the benefit of this liberty was due is now emancipated. Therefore, though they abstain from flesh and wear but one color during all the rest of their lives, this is no diminution of their freedom. Nay, because they are free, they therefore abstain with a free conscience. But they fall into a very pernicious error in disregarding the infirmity of their brethren, which it becomes us to bear, so as not rashly to do anything which would give them the least offense. But it will be said that it is sometimes right to assert our liberty before men. This I confess; yet the greatest caution and moderation must be observed lest we cast off all concern for the weak, whom God has so strongly recommended to our regards.

XI. I shall now, therefore, make some observations concerning offenses: how they are to be discriminated, what are to be avoided, and what are to be disregarded; whence we may afterwards determine what room there is for our liberty in our intercourse with mankind. I approve of the common

[14] Phil. 4:11-12.

distinction between an offense given and an offense taken, since it is plainly countenanced by Scripture, and is likewise sufficiently significant of the thing intended to be expressed. If you do anything at a wrong time or place, or with an unseasonable levity, or wantonness, or temerity, by which the weak and inexperienced are offended, it must be termed an offense given by you; because it arises from your fault. And an offense is always said to be given in any action the fault of which proceeds from the performer of that action. An offense taken is when any transaction, not otherwise unseasonable or culpable, is, through malevolence or some perverse disposition, construed into an occasion of offense. For in this instance the offense is not given, but taken, without reason by such perverseness of construction. The first species of offense affects none but the weak; the second is created by moroseness of temper and Pharisaical superciliousness. Wherefore we shall denominate the former "the offense of the weak," the latter, that "of Pharisees"! and we shall so temper the use of our liberty that it ought to submit to the ignorance of weak brethren, but not all to the austerity of Pharisees. For our duty to the weak Paul fully shows in many places. "Him that is weak in the faith receive ye." Again: "Let us not therefore judge one another any more; but judge this rather, that no man put a stumbling-block or an occasion to fall in his brother's way"; [15] and much more to the same import, which were better examined in its proper connection than recited here. The sum of all is that "we, then, that are strong, ought to bear the infirmities of the weak, and not to please ourselves. Let every one of us please his neighbor for his good to edification." [16] In another place: "But take heed lest by any means this liberty of yours become a stumbling-block to them that are weak." [17] Again: "Whatsoever is sold in the shambles, that eat, asking no questions for conscience' sake; conscience, I say, not thine own, but of the other." In short, "Give none offense, neither to the Jews nor to the Gentiles, nor to the

---

[15] Rom. 14:1, 13.   [16] Rom. 15:1-2.   [17] I Cor. 8:9.

Church of God." [18] In another place also: "Brethren, ye have been called unto liberty; only use not liberty for an occasion to the flesh, but by love serve one another." [19] The meaning of this is that our liberty is not given us to be used in opposition to our weak neighbors, to whom charity obliges us to do every possible service, but rather in order that, having peace with God in our minds, we may also live peaceably among men. But how much attention should be paid to an offense taken by Pharisees, we learn from our Lord's injunction, "Let them alone; they be blind leaders of the blind." [20] The disciples had informed him that the Pharisees were offended with his discourse. He replies that they are to be let alone, and their offense disregarded.

XII. But the subject is still pending in uncertainty unless we know whom we are to account weak, and whom we are to consider as Pharisees; without which distinction I see no use of liberty in the midst of offenses, but such as must be attended with the greatest danger. But Paul appears to me to have very clearly decided, both by doctrine and examples, how far our liberty should be either moderated or asserted on the occurrence of offenses. When he made Timothy his associate, he circumcised him, [21] but could not be induced to circumcise Titus. [22] Here was a difference in his proceedings, but no change of mind or of purpose. In the circumcision of Timothy, "though he was free from all men, yet he made himself servant unto all"; and says he, "Unto the Jews I became as a Jew, that I might gain the Jews; to them that are under the law, as under the law, that I might gain them that are under the law: I am made all things to all men, that I might by all means save some." [23] Thus we have a proper moderation of liberty, if it may be indifferently restricted with any advantage. His reason for resolutely refraining from circumcising Titus, he declares in the following words:

18 I Cor. 10:25, 29, 32. 19 Gal. 5:13.
20 Matt. 15:14. 21 Acts 16:3.
22 Gal. 2:3. 23 I Cor. 9:19-20, 22.

But neither Titus, who was with me, being a Greek, was compelled to be circumcised, and that because of false brethren unawares brought in, who came in privily to spy out our liberty which we have in Christ Jesus, that they might bring us into bondage; to whom we gave place by subjection, no, not for an hour; that the truth of the gospel might continue with you.[24]

We also are under the necessity of vindicating our liberty if it be endangered in weak consciences by the iniquitous requisitions of false apostles. We must at all times study charity, and keep in view the edification of our neighbor. "All things (says Paul) are lawful for me, but all things are not expedient: all things are lawful for me, but all things edify not. Let no man seek his own, but every man another's." [25] Nothing can be plainer than this rule that our liberty should be used if it conduces to our neighbor's edification; but that if it be not beneficial to our neighbor, it should be abridged. There are some who pretend to imitate the prudence of Paul in refraining from the exercise of liberty, while they are doing anything but exercising the duties of charity. For to promote their own tranquility, they wish all mention of liberty to be buried; whereas it is no less advantageous to our neighbors sometimes to use our liberty to their benefit and edification, than at other times to moderate it for their accommodation. But a pious man considers this liberty in external things as granted him in order that he may be the better prepared for all the duties of charity.

XIII. But whatever I have advanced respecting the avoidance of offenses, I wish to be referred to indifferent and unimportant things; for necessary duties must not be omitted through fear of any offense; as our liberty should be subject to charity, so charity itself ought to be subservient to the purity of faith. It becomes us, indeed, to have regard to charity, but we must not offend God for the love of our neighbor. We cannot approve the intemperance of those who do nothing but in a tumultuous manner, and who prefer violent measures to lenient ones. Nor must we listen to those

[24] Gal. 2:3-5.   [25] I Cor. 10:23-24.

who, while they show themselves the leaders in a thousand species of impiety, pretend that they are obliged to act in such a manner that they may give no offense to their neighbors; as though they are not at the same time fortifying the consciences of their neighbors in sin, especially since they are always sticking in the same mire without any hope of deliverance. And whether their neighbor is to be instructed by doctrine or by example, they maintain that he ought to be fed with milk, though they are infecting him with the worst and most pernicious notions. Paul tells the Corinthians, "I have fed you with milk"; [26] but if the Popish mass had been then introduced among them, would he have united in that pretended sacrifice in order to feed them with milk? Certainly not; for milk is not poison. They are guilty of falsehood, therefore, in saying that they feed those whom they cruelly murder under the appearance of such flatteries. But admitting that such dissimulation is to be approved for a time, how long will they feed their children with the same milk? For if they never grow, so as to be able to bear even some light meat, it is a clear proof that they were never fed with milk. I am prevented from pushing this controversy with them any further at present, by two reasons—first, because their absurdities scarcely deserve a refutation, being justly despised by all men of sound understanding; secondly, having done this at large in particular treatises.* I am unwilling to travel the same ground over again. Only let the readers remember that with whatever offenses Satan and the world may endeavor to divert us from the ordinances of God, or to retard our pursuit of what he enjoins, yet we must nevertheless strenuously

26 I Cor. 3:2.

* [The treatises Calvin has in mind are: *Epistolae duae de rebus . . . necessariis*, 1537; *Petit traicte, monstrant que c'est que doit faire un homme fidèle . . .* 1543; *Excuse de Jehan Calvin à Messieurs les Nicodemites*, 1544; *De vitandis superstitionibus*, 1549; *De scandalis*, 1550. Cf. Peter Barth and Wilhelm Niesel, *Joannis Calvini opera selecta*, Volume IV, Munich, 1931, p. 293. The first of these treatises is in Volume I of this series; the others will be found in the *Corpus Reformatorum* edition of Calvin's *Opera*, Volumes VI and VIII.—Ed.]

advance; and moreover, that whatever dangers threaten us, we are not at liberty to deviate even a hair's breadth from his command, and that it is not lawful under any pretext to attempt anything but what he permits.

XIV. Now, since the consciences of believers, being privileged with the liberty which we have described, have been delivered by the favor of Christ from all necessary obligation to the observance of those things in which the Lord has been pleased they should be left free, we conclude that they are exempt from all human authority. For it is not right that Christ should lose the acknowledgments due to such kindness, or our consciences the benefit of it. Neither is that to be accounted a trivial thing which we see cost Christ so much, which he estimated not with gold or silver, but with his own blood,[27] so that Paul hesitates not to assert that his death is rendered vain if we suffer our souls to be in subjection to men.[28] For his sole object in some chapters of his Epistle to the Galatians is to prove that Christ is obscured or rather abolished, with respect to us, unless our consciences continue in their liberty; from which they are certainly fallen if they can be ensnared in the bonds of laws and ordinances at the pleasure of men.[29] But as it is a subject highly worthy of being understood, so it needs a more diffuse and perspicuous explanation. For as soon as a word is mentioned concerning the abrogation of human establishments, great tumults are excited, partly by seditious persons, partly by cavillers, as though all obedience of men were at once subverted and destroyed.

XV. To prevent anyone from falling into this error, let us therefore consider, in the first place, that man is under two kinds of government—one spiritual, by which the conscience is formed to piety and the service of God; the other political, by which a man is instructed in the duties of humanity and civility, which are to be observed in an intercourse with mankind. They are generally, and not improperly, denominated the spiritual and the temporal jurisdiction, indicating

[27] I Peter 1:18-19.   [28] Gal. 5:1, 4.   [29] I Cor. 7:23.

that the former species of government pertains to the life of the soul, and that the latter relates to the concerns of the present state, not only to the provision of food and clothing, but to the enactment of laws to regulate a man's life among his neighbors by the rules of holiness, integrity, and sobriety. For the former has its seat in the interior of the mind, whilst the latter only directs the external conduct: one may be termed a spiritual kingdom, and the other a political one. But these two, as we have distinguished them, always require to be considered separately; and while the one is under discussion, the mind must be abstracted from all consideration of the other. For man contains, as it were, two worlds, capable of being governed by various rulers and various laws. This distinction will prevent what the Gospel inculcates concerning spiritual liberty from being misapplied to political regulations, as though Christians were less subject to the external government of human laws because their consciences have been set at liberty before God, as though their freedom of spirit necessarily exempted them from all carnal servitude. Again, because even in those constitutions which seem to pertain to the spiritual kingdom, there may possibly be some deception, it is necessary to discriminate between these also— which are to be accounted legitimate, as according with the Divine word, and which, on the contrary, ought not to be received among believers. Of civil government I shall treat in another place. Of ecclesiastical laws also I forbear to speak at present, because a full discussion of them will be proper in the Fourth Book, where we shall treat of the power of the Church. But we shall conclude the present argument in the following manner: the question which, as I have observed, is in itself not very obscure or intricate, greatly perplexes many because they do not distinguish with sufficient precision between the external jurisdiction and the court of conscience. The difficulty is increased by Paul's injunction to obey magistrates "not only for wrath, but also for conscience' sake," [30] from which it should follow that the conscience also is bound

30 Rom. 8:1, 5.

by political laws. But if this were true, it would supersede all that we have already said, or are now about to say, respecting spiritual government. For the solution of this difficulty it will be of use, first, to know what conscience is. And the definition of it must be derived from the etymology of the word. For as, when men apprehend the knowledge of things in the mind and understanding, they are thence said *scire*, "to know," whence is derived the word *scientia*, "science" or "knowledge," so when they have a sense of Divine justice, as an additional witness, which permits them not to conceal their sins or to elude accusation at the tribunal of the supreme Judge, this sense is termed *conscientia*, "conscience." For it is a kind of medium between God and man, because it does not suffer a man to suppress what he knows within himself, but pursues him till it brings him to conviction. This is what Paul means by "their conscience also bearing witness, and their thoughts accusing, or else excusing, one another." [31] Simple knowledge might remain, as it were, confined within a man. This sentiment, therefore, which places man before the Divine tribunal is appointed, as it were, to watch over man, to observe and examine all his secrets, that nothing may remain enveloped in darkness. Hence the old proverb, "Conscience is as a thousand witnesses." For the same reason Peter speaks of "the answer of a good conscience toward God," [32] to express our tranquility of mind when, persuaded of the favor of Christ, we present ourselves with boldness in the presence of God. And the author of the Epistle to the Hebrews expresses absolution or freedom from every future charge of sin, by "having no more conscience of sin." [33]

XVI. Therefore, as works respect men, so conscience regards God, so that a good conscience is no other than inward integrity of heart. In which sense Paul says that "the end of the commandment is charity, out of a pure heart, and of a good conscience, and of faith unfeigned." [34] Afterwards also, in the same chapter, he shows how widely it differs from un-

31 Rom. 2:15.   32 I Peter 3:21.
33 Heb. 10:2.   34 I Tim. 1:15.

derstanding, saying that "some, having put away a good conscience, concerning faith have made shipwreck." [35] For these words indicate that it is a lively inclination to the service of God and a sincere pursuit of piety and holiness of life. Sometimes, indeed, it is likewise extended to men; as when the same apostle declares, "Herein do I exercise myself, to have always a conscience void of offense toward God and toward men." [36] But the reason of this assertion is that the fruits of a good conscience reach even to men. But in strict propriety of speech it has to do with God alone, as I have already observed. Hence it is that a law which simply binds a man without relation to other men, or any consideration of them, is said to bind the conscience. For example, God not only enjoins the preservation of the mind chaste and pure from every libidinous desire, but prohibits all obscenity of language and external lasciviousness. The observance of this law is incumbent on my conscience, though there were not another man existing in the world. Thus he who transgresses the limits of temperance, not only sins by giving a bad example to his brethren, but contracts guilt on his conscience before God. Things in themselves indifferent are to be guided by other considerations. It is our duty to abstain from them if they tend to the least offense, yet without violating our liberty of conscience. So Paul speaks concerning meat consecrated to idols: "If any man say unto you, 'This is offered in sacrifice to idols,' eat not for conscience' sake—conscience, I say, not thine own, but of the other." [37] A pious man would be guilty of sin, who, being previously admonished, should nevertheless eat such meat. But though, with respect to his brother, abstinence is necessary for him, as it is enjoined by God, yet he ceases not to retain liberty of conscience. We see, then, how this law, though it binds the external action, leaves the conscience free.

[35] I Tim. 1:19.   [36] Acts 24:16.   [37] I Cor. 10:28-29.

ON CIVIL GOVERNMENT

HAVING ALREADY STATED that man is the subject of two kinds of government, and having sufficiently discussed that which is situated in the soul, or the inner man, and relates to eternal life—we are, in this chapter, to say something of the other kind which relates to civil justice and the regulation of the external conduct. For, though the nature of this argument seems to have no connection with the spiritual doctrine of faith which I have undertaken to discuss, the sequel will show that I have sufficient reason for connecting them together, and, indeed, that necessity obliges me to it, especially since, on the one hand, infatuated and barbarous men madly endeavor to subvert this ordinance established by God, and, on the other hand, the flatterers of princes, extolling their power beyond all just bounds, hesitate not to oppose it to the authority of God himself. Unless both these errors be resisted, the purity of the faith will be destroyed. Besides, it is of no small importance for us to know what benevolent provision God has made for mankind in this instance, that we may be stimulated by a greater degree of pious zeal to testify our gratitude. In the first place, before we enter on the subject itself, it is necessary for us to recur to the distinction which we have already established, lest we fall into an error very common in the world, and injudiciously confound together these two things the nature of which is altogether different. For some men, when they hear that the Gospel promises a liberty which acknowledges no king or magistrate among them, but submits to Christ alone, think they can enjoy no advantage of their liberty while they see any power exalted above them. They imagine, therefore, that nothing will prosper unless the whole world be modeled in a new form, without any tribunals or laws, or magistrates, or anything of a similar kind which they consider injurious to their liberty. But he who knows how to distinguish between the body and the soul, between this present transitory life and the future eternal one, will find no difficulty in understanding that the spiritual kingdom of Christ and civil government are things very different and remote from each other. Since it is a Jewish folly, therefore, to seek and include the kingdom of Christ under the elements of this world, let us, on the contrary, considering what the Scripture clearly inculcates, that the benefit which is received from the grace of Christ is spiritual—let us, I say, remember to confine within its proper limits all this liberty which is promised and offered to us in him. For why is it that the same apostle who, in one place, exhorts to "stand fast in the liberty wherewith Christ hath made us free and be not entangled again with the yoke of bondage," [1] in another enjoins servants to "care not for" their servile condition,[2] except that spiritual liberty may very well consist with civil servitude? In this sense we are likewise to understand him in these passages: "There is neither Jew nor Greek, there is neither bond nor free, there is neither male nor female." [3] Again: "There is neither Greek nor Jew, circumcision nor uncircumcision, Barbarian, Scythian, bond nor free: but Christ is all, and in all," [4] in which he signifies that it is of no importance what is our condition among men or under the laws of what nation we live, as the kingdom of Christ consists not in these things.

II. Yet this distinction does not lead us to consider the whole system of civil government as a polluted thing which has nothing to do with Christian men. Some fanatics who are pleased with nothing but liberty, or rather licentiousness without any restraint, do indeed boast and vociferate, That since we are dead with Christ to the elements of this world and, being translated into the kingdom of God, sit among the celestials, it is a degradation to us and far beneath our dignity to be occupied with those secular and impure cares which relate to things altogether uninteresting to a Christian man. Of what use, they ask, are laws without judgments and

1 Gal. 5:1.   2 I Cor. 7:21.
3 Gal. 3:28.   4 Col. 3:11.

tribunals? But what have judgments to do with a Christian man? And if it be unlawful to kill, of what use are laws and judgments to us? But as we have just suggested that this kind of government is distinct from that spiritual and internal reign of Christ, so it ought to be known that they are in no respect at variance with each other. For that spiritual reign, even now upon earth, commences within us some preludes of the heavenly kingdom, and in this mortal and transitory life affords us some prelibations of immortal and incorruptible blessedness; but this civil government is designed, as long as we live in this world, to cherish and support the external worship of God, to preserve the pure doctrine of religion, to defend the constitution of the Church, to regulate our lives in a manner requisite for the society of men, to form our manners to civil justice, to promote our concord with each other, and to establish general peace and tranquility—all of which I confess to be superfluous if the kingdom of God, as it now exists in us, extinguishes the present life. But if it is the will of God that while we are aspiring toward our true country, we be pilgrims on the earth, and if such aids are necessary to our pilgrimage, they who take them from man deprive him of his human nature. They plead that there should be so much perfection in the Church of God that its order would suffice to supply the place of all laws; but they foolishly imagine a perfection which can never be found in any community of men. For since the insolence of the wicked is so great, and their iniquity so obstinate, that it can scarcely be restrained by all the severity of the laws, what may we expect they would do if they found themselves at liberty to perpetuate crimes with impunity whose outrages even the arm of power cannot altogether prevent?

III. But for speaking of the exercise of civil polity, there will be another place more suitable. At present we only wish it to be understood that to entertain a thought of its extermination is inhuman barbarism; it is equally as necessary to mankind as bread and water, light and air, and far more excellent. For it not only tends to secure the accommodations arising from all these things, that men may breathe, eat, drink, and be sustained in life, though it comprehends all these things while it causes them to live together, yet I say this is not its only tendency; its objects also are that idolatry, sacrileges against the name of God, blasphemies against his truth, and other offenses against religion may not openly appear and be disseminated among the people; that the public tranquility may not be disturbed; that every person may enjoy his property without molestation; that men may transact their business together without fraud or injustice; that integrity and modesty may be cultivated among them; in short, that there may be a public form of religion among Christians, and that humanity may be maintained among men. Nor let anyone think it strange that I now refer to human polity the charge of the due maintenance of religion, which I may appear to have placed beyond the jurisdiction of men. For I do not allow men to make laws respecting religion and the worship of God now any more than I did before, though I approve of civil government which provides that the true religion contained in the law of God be not violated and polluted by public blasphemies with impunity. But the perspicuity of order will assist the readers to attain a clearer understanding of what sentiments ought to be entertained respecting the whole system of civil administration, if we enter on a discussion of each branch of it. These are three: The magistrate, who is the guardian and conservator of the laws; the laws according to which he governs; the people, who are governed by the laws and obey the magistrate. Let us, therefore, examine, first, the function of a magistrate, whether it be a legitimate calling and approved by God, the nature of the duty, and the extent of the power; secondly, by what laws Christian government ought to be regulated; and lastly, what advantage the people derive from the laws, and what obedience they owe to the magistrate.

IV. The Lord has not only testified that the function of magistrates has his approbation and acceptance, but has eminently commended it to us, by dignifying it with the most honorable titles. We will mention a few of them. When all who sustain the magistracy are called "gods," [5] it ought not to be considered as an appellation of trivial importance, for it implies that they have their command from God, that they are invested with his authority and are altogether his representatives, and act as his vicegerents. This is not an invention of mine, but the interpretation of Christ, who says, "If he called them gods, unto whom the word of God came, and the Scripture cannot be broken." [6] What is the meaning of this but that their commission has been given to them by God, to serve him in their office, and, as Moses and Jehoshaphat said to the judges whom they appointed, to "judge not for man, but for the Lord"? [7] To the same purpose is the declaration of the wisdom of God by the mouth of Solomon: "By me kings reign, and princes decree justice. By me princes rule, and nobles, even all the judges of the earth." [8] This is just as if it had been affirmed that the authority possessed by kings and other governors over all things upon earth is not a consequence of the perverseness of men but of the providence and holy ordinance of God, who has been pleased to regulate human affairs in this manner; for as much as he is present, and also presides among them, in making laws and in executing equitable judgments. This is clearly taught by Paul, when he enumerates governments (ὁ προϊστάμενος) [9] among the gifts of God, which, being variously distributed according to the diversity of grace, ought to be employed by the servants of Christ to the edification of the Church. For though in that place he is properly speaking of the council of elders, who were appointed in the primitive Church to preside over the regulation of the public discipline, the same office which in writing to the Corinthians he calls κυβέρνησις, "governments," [10] yet, as we see that civil government tends to promote the same object, there is no doubt that he recommends to us every kind of just authority. But he does this in

---

[5] Psalm 82:1, 6.
[7] Deut. 1:16-17. II Chron. 19:6.
[9] Rom. 12:8.

[6] John 10:35.
[8] Prov. 8:15-16.
[10] I Cor. 12:28.

a manner much more explicit where he enters on a full dis-cussion of that subject. For he says, "There is no power but of God; the powers that be are ordained of God. Rulers are ministers of God, revengers to execute wrath upon him that doeth evil. Do that which is good, and thou shalt have praise of the same." [11] This is corroborated by the examples of holy men, of whom some have been kings, as David, Josiah, Heze-kiah; some have been viceroys, as Joseph and Daniel; some have held civil offices in a commonwealth, as Moses, Joshua, and the Judges; whose functions God declared to be approved by him. Wherefore no doubt ought now to be entertained by any person that civil magistracy is a calling not only holy and legitimate, but far the most sacred and honorable in human life.

V. Those who would wish to introduce anarchy reply that though, in ancient times, kings and judges presided over a rude people, that servile kind of government is now quite incompatible with the perfection which accompanies the Gospel of Christ. Here they betray not only their ignorance but their diabolical pride, in boasting of perfection of which not the smallest particle can be discovered in them. But whatever their characters may be, they are easily refuted. For, when David exhorts kings and judges to kiss the Son of God,[12] he does not command them to abdicate their authority and retire to private life, but to submit to Christ the power with which they are invested, that he alone may have the pre-emi-nence over all. In like manner Isaiah, when he predicts that "kings shall be nursing-fathers and queens nursing-mothers" to the Church,[13] does not depose them from their thrones, but rather establishes them by an honorable title as patrons and protectors of the pious worshippers of God; for that prophecy relates to the advent of Christ. I purposely omit nu-merous testimonies, which often occur, and especially in the Psalms, in which the rights of all governors are asserted. But the most remarkable of all is that passage where Paul, ad-monishing Timothy that, in the public congregation, "sup-

11 Rom. 13:1, 3-4.   12 Psalm 2:10-12.   13 Isaiah 49:23.

plications, prayers, intercessions, and giving of thanks be made
for kings and for all that are in authority," assigns as a reason "that we may lead a quiet and peaceable life in all godliness and honesty" [14]—language in which he recommends the
state of the Church to their patronage and defense.

VI. This consideration ought continually to occupy the
magistrates themselves, since it is calculated to furnish them
with a powerful stimulus by which they may be excited to
their duty, and to afford them peculiar consolation by which
the difficulties of their office, which certainly are many and
arduous, may be alleviated. For what an ardent pursuit of
integrity, prudence, clemency, moderation, and innocence
ought they to prescribe to themselves who are conscious of
having been constituted ministers of the Divine justice! With
what confidence will they admit iniquity to their tribunal,
which they understand to be the throne of the living God?
With what audacity will they pronounce an unjust sentence
with that mouth which they know to be the destined organ
of Divine truth? With what conscience will they subscribe
to impious decrees with that hand which they know to be appointed to register the edicts of God? In short, if they remember that they are the vicegerents of God, it behooves them
to watch with all care, earnestness, and diligence, that in their
administration they may exhibit to men an image, as it were,
of the providence, care, goodness, benevolence, and justice
of God. And they must constantly bear this in mind that if
in all cases "he be cursed that doeth the work of the Lord
deceitfully," [15] a far heavier curse awaits those who act fraudulently in a righteous calling. Therefore, when Moses and
Jehoshaphat wished to exhort their judges to the discharge of
their duty, they had nothing to suggest more efficacious than
the principle which we have already mentioned. Moses says,
"Judge righteously between every man and his brother, and
the stranger that is with him. For the judgment is God's." [16]
Jehoshaphat says, "Take heed what ye do; for ye judge not
for man, but for the Lord, who is with you in the judgment.

14 I Tim. 2:1-2.   15 Jer. 47:10.   16 Deut. 1:16-17.

Wherefore now let the fear of the Lord be upon you: take heed and do it; for there is no iniquity with the Lord our God." [17] And in another place it is said, "God standeth in the congregation of the mighty: he judgeth among the gods"; [18] that they may be animated to their duty when they understand that they are delegated by God, to whom they must one day render an account of their administration. And this admonition is entitled to have considerable weight with them; for if they fail in their duty, they not only injure men by criminally distressing them, but even offend God by polluting his sacred judgments. On the other hand, it opens a source of peculiar consolation to them to reflect that they are not employed in profane things, or occupations unsuitable to a servant of God, but in a most sacred function, inasmuch as they execute a Divine commission.

VII. Those who are not restrained by so many testimonies of Scripture, but still dare to stigmatize this sacred ministry as a thing incompatible with religion and Christian piety, do they not offer an insult to God himself, who cannot but be involved in the reproach cast upon his ministry? And in fact they do not reject magistrates, but they reject God, "that he should not reign over them." [19] For if this was truly asserted by the Lord respecting the people of Israel, because they refused the government of Samuel, why shall it not now be affirmed with equal truth of those who take the liberty to outrage all the authorities which God has instituted? But they object that our Lord said to his disciples, "The kings of the Gentiles exercise lordship over them, but ye shall not be so; but he that is greatest among you, let him be as the younger; and he that is chief, as he that doth serve:" [20] and they contend that these words prohibit the exercise of royalty or any other authority by any Christians. Admirable expositors! A contention had arisen among the disciples "which of them should be accounted the greatest." To repress this vain ambition, our Lord taught them that their ministry was not like

[17] II Chron. 19:6-7.
[19] I Sam. 8:7.
[18] Psalm 82:1.
[20] Luke 22:25-26.

temporal kingdoms, in which one person has the pre-eminence over all others. Now, what dishonor does this comparison cast upon regal dignity? What does it prove at all, except that the regal office is not the apostolic ministry? Moreover, though there are various forms of magistracy, yet there is no difference in this respect, but we ought to receive them all as ordinances of God. For Paul comprehends them all together when he says that "there is no power but of God"; and that which was furthest from giving general satisfaction is recommended to us in a remarkable manner beyond all others—namely, the government of one man, which, as it is attended with the common servitude of all, except the single individual to whose will all others are subjected, has never been so highly approved by heroic and noble minds. But the Scripture, on the contrary, to correct these unjust sentiments, expressly affirms that it is by the providence of Divine wisdom that kings reign, and particularly commands us to "honor the king." [21]

VIII. And for private men, who have no authority to deliberate on the regulation of any public affairs, it would surely be a vain occupation to dispute which would be the best form of government in the place where they live. Besides, this could not be simply determined, as an abstract question, without great impropriety, since the principle to guide the decision must depend on circumstances. And even if we compare the different forms together, without their circumstances, their advantages are so nearly equal that it will not be easy to discover of which the utility preponderates. The forms of civil government are considered to be of three kinds: Monarchy, which is the dominion of one person, whether called a king or a duke, or any other title; Aristocracy, or the dominion of the principal persons of a nation; and Democracy, or popular government, in which the power resides in the people at large. It is true that the transition is easy from monarchy to despotism; it is not much more difficult from aristocracy to oligarchy, or the faction of a few; but it is most easy of all from democracy to sedition. Indeed, if these three forms of

21 Rom. 13:1f. Prov. 8:15. I Pet. 2:13-14, 17.

government which are stated by philosophers be considered in themselves, I shall by no means deny that either aristocracy or a mixture of aristocracy and democracy far excels all others; and that indeed not of itself, but because it very rarely happens that kings regulate themselves so that their will is never at variance with justice and rectitude; or, in the next place, that they are endued with such penetration and prudence as in all cases to discover what is best. The vice or imperfection of men therefore renders it safer and more tolerable for the government to be in the hands of many, that they may afford each other mutual assistance and admonition, and that if any one arrogate to himself more than is right, the many may act as censors and masters to restrain his ambition. This has always been proved by experience, and the Lord confirmed it by his authority when he established a government of this kind among the people of Israel, with a view to preserve them in the most desirable condition till he exhibited in David a type of Christ. And as I readily acknowledge that no kind of government is more happy than this where liberty is regulated with becoming moderation and properly established on a durable basis, so also I consider those as the most happy people who are permitted to enjoy such a condition; and if they exert their strenuous and constant efforts for its preservation and retention, I admit that they act in perfect consistence with their duty. And to this object the magistrates likewise ought to apply their greatest diligence, that they suffer not the liberty, of which they are constituted guardians, to be in any respect diminished, much less to be violated; if they are inactive and unconcerned about this, they are perfidious to their office, and traitors to their country. But if those to whom the will of God has assigned another form of government transfer this to themselves so as to be tempted to desire a revolution, the very thought will be not only foolish and useless, but altogether criminal. If we limit not our views to one city, but look round and take a comprehensive survey of the whole world, or at least extend our observations to distant lands, we shall certainly find it to

be a wise arrangement of Divine Providence that various countries are governed by different forms of civil polity, for they
are admirably held together with a certain inequality, as the
elements are combined in very unequal proportions. All these
remarks, however, will be unnecessary to those who are satisfied with the will of the Lord. For if it be his pleasure to appoint kings over kingdoms, and senators or other magistrates
over free cities, it is our duty to be obedient to any governors whom God has established over the places in which we
reside.

IX. Here it is necessary to state in a brief manner the nature of the office of magistracy, as described in the word of
God, and wherein it consists. If the Scripture did not teach
that this office extends to both tables of the law, we might
learn it from heathen writers; for not one of them has treated
of the office of magistrates, of legislation, and civil government, without beginning with religion and Divine worship.
And thus they have all confessed that no government can be
happily constituted unless its first object be the promotion
of piety, and that all laws are preposterous which neglect the
claims of God and merely provide for the interests of men.
Therefore, as religion holds the first place among all the philosophers, and as this has always been regarded by the universal consent of all nations, Christian princes and magistrates
ought to be ashamed of their indolence if they do not make
it the object of their most serious care. We have already shown
that this duty is particularly enjoined upon them by God; for
it is reasonable that they should employ their utmost efforts
in asserting and defending the honor of Him whose vicegerents they are and by whose favor they govern. And the
principal commendations given in the Scripture to the good
kings are for having restored the worship of God when it
had been corrupted or abolished, or for having devoted their
attention to religion, that it might flourish in purity and
safety under their reigns. On the contrary, the sacred history
represents it as one of the evils arising from anarchy, or a
want of good government, that when "there was no king in

Israel, every man did that which was right in his own eyes." [22] These things evince the folly of those who would wish magistrates to neglect all thoughts of God, and to confine themselves entirely to the administration of justice among men, as though God appointed governors in his name to decide secular controversies, and disregarded that which is of far greater importance—the pure worship of himself according to the rule of his law. But a rage for universal innovation, and a desire to escape with impunity, instigate men of turbulent spirits to wish that all the avengers of violated piety were removed out of the world. With respect to the second table, Jeremiah admonishes kings in the following manner: "Execute ye judgment and righteousness, and deliver the spoiled out of the hand of the oppressor; and do no wrong, do no violence to the stranger, the fatherless, nor the widow, neither shed innocent blood." [23] To the same purpose is the exhortation in the eighty-second psalm: "Defend the poor and fatherless: do justice to the afflicted and needy: deliver the poor and needy: rid them out of the hand of the wicked." [24] And Moses "charged the judges" whom he appointed to supply his place, saying—

Hear the causes between your brethren, and judge righteously between every man and his brother, and the stranger that is with him: ye shall not respect persons in judgment; but ye shall hear the small as well as the great; ye shall not be afraid of the face of man; for the judgment is God's.[25]

I forbear to remark the directions given by him in another place respecting their future kings: "He shall not multiply horses to himself; neither shall he greatly multiply to himself silver and gold; his heart shall not be lifted up above his brethren; he shall read in the law all the days of his life"; [26] also that judges show no partiality nor take bribes, with similar injunctions, which abound in the Scriptures; because, in describing the office of magistrates in this treatise, my design

22 Judges 21:25.   23 Jer. 22:3.
24 Psalm 82:3-4.   25 Deut. 1:16-17.
26 Deut. 17:16-17, 19-20.

is not so much to instruct magistrates themselves, as to show to others what magistrates are and for what end God has appointed them. We see, therefore, that they are constituted the protectors and vindicators of the public innocence, modesty, probity, and tranquility, whose sole object it ought to be to promote the common peace and security of all. Of these virtues, David declares that he will be an example when he shall be exalted to the royal throne.

I will set no wicked thing before mine eyes. I will not know a wicked person. Whoso privily slandereth his neighbour, him will I cut off: him that hath a high look and a proud heart will I not suffer. Mine eyes shall be upon the faithful of the land, that they may dwell with me: he that walketh in a perfect way, he shall serve me.[27]

But as they cannot do this unless they defend good men from the injuries of the wicked and aid the oppressed by their relief and protection, they are likewise armed with power for the suppression of crimes, and the severe punishment of malefactors whose wickedness disturbs the public peace. For experience fully verifies the observation of Solon: "That all states are supported by reward and punishment; and that when these two things are removed, all the discipline of human societies is broken and destroyed." For the minds of many lose their regard for equity and justice unless virtue be rewarded with due honor; nor can the violence of the wicked be restrained unless crimes are followed by severe punishments. And these two parts are included in the injunction of the prophet to kings and other governors to "execute judgment and righteousness." [28] "Righteousness" means the care, patronage, defense, vindication, and liberation of the innocent; "judgment" imports the repression of the audacity, the coercion of the violence, and the punishment of the crime of the impious.

X. But here, it seems, arises an important and difficult question. If by the law of God all Christians are forbidden to kill,[29] and the prophet predicts respecting the Church that

[27] Psalm 101:3-6.   [28] Jer. 22:3.   [29] Exod. 20:13.

"they shall not hurt nor destroy in all my holy mountain, saith the Lord," [30] how can it be compatible with piety for magistrates to shed blood? But if we understand that in the infliction of punishments the magistrate does not act at all from himself, but merely executes the judgments of God, we shall not be embarrassed with this scruple. The law of the Lord commands, "Thou shalt not kill"; but that homicide may not go unpunished, the legislator himself puts the sword into the hands of his ministers, to be used against all homicides.[31] *To hurt* and *to destroy* are incompatible with the character of the godly; but to avenge the afflictions of the righteous at the command of God is neither *to hurt* nor *to destroy*. Therefore it is easy to conclude that in this respect magistrates are not subject to the common law, by which, though the Lord binds the hands of men, he does not bind his own justice, which he exercises by the hands of magistrates. So, when a prince forbids all his subjects to strike or wound anyone, he does not prohibit his officers from executing that justice which is particularly committed to them. I sincerely wish that this consideration were constantly in our recollection, that nothing is done here by the temerity of men, but everything by the authority of God, who commands it, and under whose guidance we never err from the right way. For we can find no valid objection to the infliction of public vengeance unless the justice of God be restrained from the punishment of crimes. But if it be unlawful for us to impose restraints upon him, why do we calumniate his ministers? Paul says of the magistrate that "He beareth not the sword in vain; for he is the minister of God, a revenger to execute wrath upon him that doeth evil." [32] Therefore, if princes and other governors know that nothing will be more acceptable to God than their obedience, and if they desire to approve their piety, justice, and integrity before God, let them devote themselves to this duty. This motive influenced Moses when, knowing himself to be destined to become the liberator of

---

[30] Isaiah 11:9; 65:25.   [31] Gen. 9:6. Exod. 21:12.   [32] Rom. 13:4.

his people by the power of the Lord, "he slew the Egyptian"; [33] and when he punished the idolatry of the people by the slaughter of three thousand men in one day.[34] The same motive actuated David when, at the close of his life, he commanded his son Solomon to put to death Joab and Shimei.[35] Hence, also, it is enumerated among the virtues of a king to "destroy all the wicked of the land, that he may cut off all wicked doers from the city of the Lord." [36] The same topic furnishes the eulogium given to Solomon: "Thou lovest righteousness, and hatest wickedness." [37] How did the meek and placid disposition of Moses burn with such cruelty that, after having his hands imbrued in the blood of his brethren, he continued to go through the camp till three thousand were slain? How did David, who discovered such humanity all his lifetime, in his last moments bequeath such a cruel injunction to his son respecting Joab? "Let not his hoarhead go down to the grave in peace"; and respecting Shimei: "His hoarhead bring down to the grave with blood." Both Moses and David, in executing the vengeance committed to them by God, by this severity sanctified their hands, which would have been defiled by lenity. Solomon says, "It is an abomination to kings to commit wickedness; for the throne is established by righteousness." [38] Again: "A king that sitteth in the throne of judgment, scattereth away all evil with his eyes." [39] Again: "A wise king scattereth the wicked, and bringeth the wheel over them." [40] Again: "Take away the dross from the silver, and there shall come forth a vessel for the finer. Take away the wicked from before the king, and his throne shall be established in righteousness." [41] Again: "He that justifieth the wicked, and he that condemneth the just, even they both are an abomination to the Lord." [42] Again: "An evil man seeketh only rebellion; therefore a cruel messenger shall be sent

[33] Exod. 2:12.
[35] I Kings 2:5-9.
[37] Psalm 45:7.
[39] Prov. 20:8.
[41] Prov. 25:4-5.

[34] Exod. 32:26-28.
[36] Psalm 101:8.
[38] Prov. 16:12.
[40] Prov. 20:26.
[42] Prov. 17:15.

against him." [43] Again: "He that saith unto the wicked, Thou art righteous; him shall the people curse, nations shall abhor him." [44] Now, if it be true justice for them to pursue the wicked with a drawn sword, let them sheathe the sword and keep their hands from shedding blood while the swords of desperadoes are drenched in murders, and they will be so far from acquiring the praise of goodness and justice by this forbearance that they will involve themselves in the deepest impiety. There ought not, however, to be any excessive or unreasonable severity, nor ought any cause to be given for considering the tribunal as a gibbet prepared for all who are accused. For I am not an advocate for unnecessary cruelty, nor can I conceive the possibility of an equitable sentence being pronounced without mercy; of which Solomon affirms that "mercy and truth preserve the king; and his throne is upholden by mercy." [45] Yet it behooves the magistrate to be on his guard against both these errors—that he do not, by excessive severity, wound rather than heal, or, through a superstitious affectation of clemency, fall into a mistaken humanity, which is the worst kind of cruelty, by indulging a weak and ill-judged lenity to the detriment of multitudes. For it is a remark not without foundation that was anciently applied to the government of Nerva, that it is bad to live under a prince who permits nothing, but much worse to live under one who permits everything.

XI. Now, as it is sometimes necessary for kings and nations to take up arms for the infliction of such public vengeance, the same reason will lead us to infer the lawfulness of wars which are undertaken for this end. For if they have been entrusted with power to preserve the tranquility of their own territories, to suppress the seditious tumults of disturbers, to succor the victims of oppression, and to punish crimes —can they exert this power for a better purpose than to repel the violence of him who disturbs both the private repose of individuals and the general tranquility of the nation, who excites insurrections and perpetrates acts of oppression, cruelty,

[43] Prov. 17:11. [44] Prov. 24:24. [45] Prov. 20:28.

and every species of crime? If they ought to be the guardians and defenders of the laws, it is incumbent upon them to defeat the efforts of all by whose injustice the discipline of the laws is corrupted. And if they justly punish those robbers whose injuries have only extended to a few persons, shall they suffer a whole district to be plundered and devastated with impunity? For there is no difference whether he who in a hostile manner invades, disturbs, and plunders the territory of another to which he has no right be a king or one of the meanest of mankind: all persons of this description are equally to be considered as robbers, and ought to be punished as such. It is the dictate both of natural equity and of the nature of the office, therefore, that princes are armed, not only to restrain the crimes of private individuals by judicial punishments, but also to defend the territories committed to their charge by going to war against any hostile aggression; and the Holy Spirit, in many passages of Scripture, declares such wars to be lawful.

XII. If it be objected that the New Testament contains no precept or example which proves war to be lawful to Christians, I answer, first, that the reason for waging war which existed in ancient times is equally valid in the present age; and that, on the contrary, there is no cause to prevent princes from defending their subjects. Secondly, that no express declaration on this subject is to be expected in the writings of the apostles, whose design was not to organize civil governments, but to describe the spiritual kingdom of Christ. Lastly, that in those very writings it is implied, by the way, that no change has been made in this respect by the coming of Christ. "For," to use the words of Augustine,

if Christian discipline condemned all wars, the soldiers who inquired respecting their salvation ought rather to have been directed to cast away their arms, and entirely to renounce the military profession; whereas the advice given them was, "Do violence to no man, neither accuse any falsely; and be content with your wages." [46] An injunction to be content with

46 Luke 3:14.

their wages was certainly not a prohibition of the military life.*

But here all magistrates ought to be very cautious, that they follow not in any respect the impulse of their passions. On the contrary, if punishments are to be inflicted, they ought not to be precipitated with anger, exasperated with hatred, or inflamed with implacable severity; they ought, as Augustine says, "to commiserate our common nature even in him whom they punish for his crime." Or, if arms are to be resorted to against an enemy, that is, an armed robber, they ought not to seize a trivial occasion, nor even to take it when presented, unless they are driven to it by extreme necessity. For, if it be our duty to exceed what was required by that heathen writer who maintained that the evident object of war ought to be the restoration of peace,† certainly we ought to make every other attempt before we have recourse to the decision of arms. In short, in both cases they must not suffer themselves to be carried away by any private motive, but be wholly guided by public spirit; otherwise they grossly abuse their power, which is given them, not for their own particular advantage, but for the benefit and service of others. Moreover, on this right of war depends the lawfulness of garrisons, alliances, and other civil munitions. By "garrisons," I mean soldiers who are stationed in towns to defend the boundaries of a country. By "alliances," I mean confederations which are made between neighboring princes, that, if any disturbance arise in their territories, they will render each other mutual assistance, and will unite their forces together for the common resistance of the common enemies of mankind. By "civil munitions," I mean all the provisions which are employed in the art of war.

XIII. In the last place, I think it necessary to add that tributes and taxes are the legitimate revenues of princes; which, indeed, they ought principally to employ in sustaining the public expenses of their office, but which they may likewise use for the support of their domestic splendor, which is closely

* [Cf. Augustinus, *Epist. 5, ad. Marcellinum.*]
† [Plato, *Laws* 628d.]

connected with the dignity of the government that they hold.
Thus we see that David, Jehoshaphat, Hezekiah, Josiah, and
other pious kings, and likewise Joseph and Daniel, without
any violation of piety, on account of the office which they
filled, lived at the public expense; and we read in Ezekiel
of a very ample portion of land being assigned to the kings; [47]
in which passage, though the prophet is describing the spiritual kingdom of Christ, yet he borrows the model of it from
the legitimate kingdoms of men. On the other hand, princes
themselves ought to remember that their finances are not so
much private incomes as the revenues of the whole people,
according to the testimony of Paul,[48] and therefore cannot be
lavished or dilapidated without manifest injustice; or, rather,
that they are to be considered as the blood of the people, not
to spare which is the most inhuman cruelty; and their various
imposts and tributes ought to be regarded merely as aids of
the public necessity, to burden the people with which, without cause, would be tyrannical rapacity. These things give no
encouragement to princes to indulge profusion and luxury;
and certainly there is no need to add fuel to their passions,
which of themselves are more than sufficiently inflamed; but,
as it is of very great importance that whatever they undertake they attempt it with a pure conscience before God, it is
necessary, in order to their avoiding vain confidence and contempt of God, that they be taught how far their rights extend.
Nor is this doctrine useless to private persons, who learn from
it not to pronounce rash and insolent censures on the expenses of princes, notwithstanding they exceed the limits of
common life.

XIV. From the magistracy, we next proceed to the laws,
which are the strong nerves of civil polity, or, according to an
appellation which Cicero has borrowed from Plato, the "souls
of states," without which magistracy cannot subsist, as, on the
other hand, without magistrates laws are of no force. No observation, therefore, can be more correct than this that the
law is a silent magistrate, and a magistrate a speaking law.

47 Ezek. 48:21-22.   48 Rom. 13:6.

Though I have promised to show by what laws a Christian state ought to be regulated, it will not be reasonable for any person to expect a long discussion respecting the best kind of laws; which is a subject of immense extent, and foreign from our present object. I will briefly remark, however, by the way, what laws it may piously use before God, and be rightly governed by among men. And even this I would have preferred passing over in silence if I did not know that it is a point on which many persons run into dangerous errors. For some deny that a state is well constituted which neglects the polity of Moses and is governed by the common laws of nations. The dangerous and seditious nature of this opinion I leave to the examination of others; it will be sufficient for me to have evinced it to be false and foolish. Now, it is necessary to observe that common distinction which distributes all the laws of God promulgated by Moses into moral, ceremonial, and judicial; and these different kinds of laws are to be distinctly examined, that we may ascertain what belongs to us, and what does not. Nor let anyone be embarrassed by this scruple that even the ceremonial and judicial precepts are included in the moral. For the ancients, who first made this distinction, were not ignorant that these two kinds of precepts related to the conduct of moral agents, yet, as they might be changed and abrogated without affecting the morality of actions, therefore they did not call them moral precepts. They particularly applied this appellation to those precepts without which there can be no real purity of morals, nor any permanent rule of a holy life.

XV. The moral law, therefore, with which I shall begin, being comprised in two leading articles, of which one simply commands us to worship God with pure faith and piety, and the other enjoins us to embrace men with sincere love—this law, I say, is the true and eternal rule of righteousness, prescribed to men of all ages and nations who wish to conform their lives to the will of God. For this is his eternal and immutable will that he himself be worshipped by us all, and that we mutually love one another. The ceremonial law was the pupilage of the Jews, with which it pleased the Lord to exercise that people during a state resembling childhood, till that "fullness of the time" should come [49] when he would fully manifest his wisdom to the world and would exhibit the reality of those things which were then adumbrated in figures. The judicial law, given to them as a political constitution, taught them certain rules of equity and justice by which they might conduct themselves in a harmless and peaceable manner toward each other. And as that exercise of ceremonies properly related to the doctrine of piety, inasmuch as it kept the Jewish Church in the worship and service of God, which is the first article of the moral law, and yet was distinct from piety itself, so these judicial regulations, though they had no other end than the preservation of that love which is enjoined in the eternal law of God, yet had something which distinguished them from that precept itself. As the ceremonies, therefore, might be abrogated without any violation or injury of piety, so the precepts and duties of love remain of perpetual obligation, notwithstanding the abolition of all these judicial ordinances. If this be true, certainly all nations are left at liberty to enact such laws as they shall find to be respectively expedient for them, provided they be framed according to that perpetual rule of love, so that, though they vary in form, they may have the same end. For those barbarous and savage laws which rewarded theft and permitted promiscuous concubinage, with others still more vile, execrable, and absurd, I am very far from thinking ought to be considered as laws; since they are not only violations of all righteousness, but outrages against humanity itself.

XVI. What I have said will be more clearly understood if in all laws we properly consider these two things—the constitution of the law and its equity, on the reason of which the constitution itself is founded and rests. Equity, being natural, is the same to all mankind; and consequently all laws, on every subject, ought to have the same equity for their end. Particular enactments and regulations, being connected with

[49] Gal. 3:24; 4:4.

circumstances, and partly dependent upon them, may be different in different cases without any impropriety, provided they are all equally directed to the same object of equity. Now, as it is certain that the law of God, which we call the moral law, is no other than a declaration of natural law, and of that conscience which has been engraven by God on the minds of men, the whole rule of this equity, of which we now speak, is prescribed in it. This equity, therefore, must alone be the scope and rule and end of all laws. Whatever laws shall be framed according to that rule, directed to that object, and limited to that end, there is no reason why we should censure them, however they may differ from the Jewish law or from each other. The law of God forbids theft. What punishment was enacted for thieves among the Jews may be seen in the book of Exodus.[50] The most ancient laws of other nations punished theft by requiring a compensation of double the value. Subsequent laws made a distinction between open and secret theft. Some proceeded to banishment, some to flagellation, and some to the punishment of death. False witness was punished among the Jews with the same punishment as such testimony would have caused to be inflicted on the person against whom it was given; [51] in some countries it was punished with infamy, in others with hanging, in others with crucifixion. All laws agree in punishing murder with death, though in several different forms. The punishments of adulterers in different countries have been attended with different degrees of severity. Yet we see how, amidst this diversity, they are all directed to the same end. For they all agree in denouncing punishment against those crimes which are condemned by the eternal law of God; such as murders, thefts, adulteries, false testimonies, though there is not a uniformity in the mode of punishment; and, indeed, this is neither necessary, nor even expedient. One country, if it did not inflict the most exemplary vengeance upon murderers, would soon be ruined by murders and robberies. One age requires the severity of punishments to be increased. If a country be dis-

50 Exod. 22:1f.   51 Deut. 19:18-19.

turbed by any civil commotion, the evils which generally arise from it must be corrected by new edicts. In time of war all humanity would be forgotten amidst the din of arms if men were not awed by more than a common dread of punishment. During famine and pestilence, unless greater severity be employed, everything will fall into ruin. One nation is more prone than others to some particular vice unless it be most rigidly restrained. What malignity and envy against the public good will be betrayed by him who shall take offense at such diversity, which is best adapted to secure the observance of the law of God! For the objection made by some, that it is an insult to the law of God given by Moses when it is abrogated and other laws are preferred to it, is without any foundation; for neither are other laws preferred to it when they are more approved, not on a simple comparison, but on account of the circumstances of time, place, and nation, nor do we abrogate that which was never given to us. For the Lord gave not that law by the hand of Moses to be promulgated among all nations, and to be universally binding; but after having taken the Jewish nation into his special charge, patronage, and protection, he was pleased to become, in a peculiar manner, their legislator, and, as became a wise legislator, in all the laws which he gave them he had a special regard to their peculiar circumstances.

XVII. It now remains for us, as we proposed, in the last place, to examine what advantage the common society of Christians derives from laws, judgments, and magistrates; with which is connected another question—what honor private persons ought to render to magistrates, and how far their obedience ought to extend. Many persons suppose the office of magistracy to be of no use among Christians, for that they cannot, consistently with piety, apply for their assistance because they are forbidden to have recourse to revenge or litigation. But as Paul, on the contrary, clearly testifies that the magistrate is "the minister of God to us for good," [52] we understand from this that he is divinely appointed, in order that

52 Rom. 13:4.

we may be defended by his power and protection against the malice and injuries of wicked men, and may lead peaceable and secure lives. But if it be in vain that he is given to us by the Lord for our protection, unless it be lawful for us to avail ourselves of such an advantage, it clearly follows that we may appeal to him and apply for his aid without any violation of piety. But here I have to do with two sorts of persons; for there are multitudes inflamed with such a rage for litigation that they never have peace in themselves unless they are in contention with others; and they commence their lawsuits with a mortal bitterness of animosities and with an infuriated cupidity of revenge and injury, and pursue them with an implacable obstinacy, even to the ruin of their adversary. At the same time, that they may not be thought to do anything wrong, they defend this perverseness under the pretext of seeking justice. But, though it is allowable for a man to endeavor to obtain justice from his neighbor by a judicial process, he is not therefore at liberty to hate him or to cherish a desire to hurt him, or to persecute him without mercy.

XVIII. Let such persons, therefore, understand that judicial processes are lawful to those who use them rightly; and that the right use, both for the plaintiff and for the defendant, is this: First, if the plaintiff, being injured either in his person or in his property, has recourse to the protection of the magistrate, states his complaint, makes a just and equitable claim, but without any desire of injury or revenge, without any asperity or hatred, without any ardor for contention, but rather prepared to waive his right and to sustain some disadvantage than to cherish enmity against his adversary. Secondly, if the defendant, being summoned, appears on the day appointed and defends his cause by the best arguments in his power, without any bitterness, but with the simple desire of maintaining his just right. On the contrary, when their minds are filled with malevolence, corrupted with envy, incensed with wrath, stimulated with revenge, or inflamed with the fervor of contention, so as to diminish their charity, all the proceedings of the justest cause are inevitably wicked. For it ought to be an established maxim with all Christians that, however just a cause may be, no lawsuit can ever be carried on in a proper manner by any man who does not feel as much benevolence and affection toward his adversary, as if the business in dispute had already been settled and terminated by an amicable adjustment. Some, perhaps, will object that such moderation in lawsuits is far from being ever practiced, and that if one instance of it were to be found, it would be regarded as a prodigy. I confess, indeed, that, in the corruption of these times, the example of an upright litigator is very rare; but the thing itself ceases not to be good and pure if it be not defiled by an adventitious evil. But when we hear that the assistance of the magistrate is a holy gift of God, it behooves us to use the more assiduous caution, that it be not contaminated by our guilt.

XIX. Those who positively condemn all controversies at law ought to understand that they thereby reject a holy ordinance of God, and a gift of the number of those which may be "pure to the pure," unless they mean to charge Paul with a crime, who repelled the calumnies of his accusers, exposing their subtlety and malice; who, before his judges, asserted his right to the privileges of a Roman citizen; and who, when he found it necessary, appealed from an unjust governor to the tribunal of Caesar. It is no objection to this that all Christians are forbidden the desire of revenge, which we also wish to banish to the greatest distance from all Christian judicatures. For, in a civil cause, no man proceeds in the right way who does not, with innocent simplicity, commit his cause to the judge as to a public guardian, without the least thought of a mutual retaliation of evil, which is the passion of revenge. And in any more important or criminal action we require the accuser to be one who goes into the court, influenced by no desire of revenge, affected by no resentment of private injury, and having no other motive than to resist the attempts of a mischievous man, that he may not injure the public. But if a vindictive spirit be excluded, no offense is committed against that precept by which revenge is forbidden to Christians. It may probably be objected that they are not only forbidden to desire revenge, but are also commanded to wait for the hand of the Lord, who promises that he will assist and revenge the afflicted and oppressed, and, therefore, that those who seek the interference of the magistrate on behalf of themselves or others anticipate all that vengeance of the celestial protector. But this is very far from the truth. For the vengeance of the magistrate is to be considered, not as the vengeance of man, but of God, which, according to the testimony of Paul, he exercises by the ministry of men for our good.

XX. Nor do we any more oppose the prohibition and injunction of Christ, "Resist not evil; but whosoever shall smite thee on thy right cheek, turn to him the other also; and if any man will sue thee at the law, and take away thy coat, let him have thy cloak also." [53] In this passage, indeed, he requires the minds of his servants to be so far from cherishing a desire of retaliation, as rather to suffer the repetition of an injury against themselves than to wish to revenge it; nor do we dissuade them from this patience. For it truly behooves Christians to be a people, as it were, formed to bear injuries and reproaches, exposed to the iniquity, impostures, and ridicule of the worst of mankind; and not only so, but they ought to be patient under all these evils; that is to say, so calm and composed in their minds that, after having suffered one affliction, they may prepare themselves for another, expecting nothing all their lifetime but to bear a perpetual cross. At the same time, they are required to bless and pray for them from whom they receive curses, to do good to them from whom they experience injuries,[54] and to aim at that which constitutes their only victory, to "overcome evil with good." [55] With this disposition they will not demand "an eye for an eye, and a tooth for a tooth," as the Pharisees taught their disciples to desire revenge; but, as we are instructed by Christ, they will suffer injuries in their persons and property in such a manner as to be ready to forgive them as soon as

[53] Matt. 5:39-40.   [54] Matt. 5:44.   [55] Rom. 12:21.

they are committed.[56] Yet this equanimity and moderation
will be no obstacle but that, without any breach of friend-
ship toward their enemies, they may avail themselves of the
assistance of the magistrate for the preservation of their property, or, from zeal for the public good, may bring a pestilent
offender to justice, though they know he can only be punished with death. For it is very correctly explained by Augustine that the end of all these precepts is—

that a just and pious man should be ready to bear with patience the wickedness of those whom he desires to become
good; rather in order that the number of the good may increase, not that with similar wickedness he may himself join
the number of the evil; and in the next place, that they relate
to the internal affection of the heart more than to the external
actions; in order that in the secrecy of our minds we may feel
patience and benevolence, but in our outward conduct may
do that which we see tends to the advantage of those to whom
we ought to feel benevolent affections.*

XXI. The objection which is frequently alleged, that lawsuits are universally condemned by Paul, has no foundation
in truth.[57] It may be easily understood from his words that
in the Church of the Corinthians there was an immoderate
rage for litigation, so that they exposed the Gospel of Christ,
and all the religion which they professed, to the cavils and
reproaches of the impious. The first thing which Paul repre-
hended in them was that the intemperance of their dissensions brought the Gospel into discredit among unbelievers.
And the next thing was that they had such altercations among
them, brethren with brethren, for they were so far from bearing an injury that they coveted each other's property and
molested and injured one another without any provocation.
It was against that rage for litigation, therefore, that he in-
veighed, and not absolutely against all controversies. But he
pronounces it to be altogether a vice or a weakness that they
did not suffer the injury or loss of their property rather than
to proceed to contentions for the preservation of it; when

56 Matt. 5:38-40.　　* [Augustinus, *Epist. 5, ad Marcellinum.*]
57 I Cor. 6:1-8.

they were so disturbed or exasperated at every loss or injury that they had recourse to lawsuits on the most trivial occasions, he argues that this proved their minds to be too irritable and not sufficiently patient. It is certainly incumbent on Christians, in all cases, to prefer a concession of their right to an entrance on a lawsuit; from which they can scarcely come out without a mind exasperated and inflamed with enmity to their brother. But when one sees that, without any breach of charity, he may defend his property the loss of which would be a serious injury to him—if he do it, he commits no offense against that sentence of Paul. In a word, as we have observed at the beginning, charity will give everyone the best counsel; for, whatever litigations are undertaken without charity, or are carried to a degree inconsistent with it, we conclude them, beyond all controversy, to be unjust and wicked.

XXII. The first duty of subjects toward their magistrates is to entertain the most honorable sentiments of their function, which they know to be a jurisdiction delegated to them from God, and on that account to esteem and reverence them as God's ministers and vicegerents. For there are some persons to be found who show themselves very obedient to their magistrates and have not the least wish that there were no magistrates for them to obey, because they know them to be so necessary to the public good, but who, nevertheless, consider the magistrates themselves as no other than necessary evils. But something more than this is required of us by Peter when he commands us to "honor the king"; [58] and by Solomon, when he says, "Fear thou the Lord and the king"; [59] for Peter, under the term "honor," comprehends a sincere and candid esteem; and Solomon, by connecting the king with the Lord, attributes to him a kind of sacred veneration and dignity. It is also a remarkable commendation of magistrates which is given by Paul, when he says that we "must needs be subject, not only for wrath, but also for conscience' sake"; [60] by which he means that subjects ought to be induced to sub-

[58] I Peter 2:17. [59] Prov. 24:21. [60] Rom. 13:5.

mit to princes and governors, not merely from a dread of their power, as persons are accustomed to yield to an armed enemy, who they know will immediately take vengeance upon them if they resist; but because the obedience which is rendered to princes and magistrates is rendered to God, from whom they have received their authority. I am not speaking of the persons as if the mask of dignity ought to palliate or excuse folly, ignorance, or cruelty, and conduct the most nefarious and flagitious, and so to acquire for vices the praise due to virtues; but I affirm that the station itself is worthy of honor and reverence, so that, whoever our governors are, they ought to possess our esteem and veneration on account of the office which they fill.

XXIII. Hence follows another duty—that, with minds disposed to honor and reverence magistrates, subjects approve their obedience to them in submitting to their edicts, in paying taxes, in discharging public duties, and bearing burdens which relate to the common defense, and in fulfilling all their other commands. Paul says to the Romans, "Let every soul be subject unto the higher powers. Whosoever resisteth the power, resisteth the ordinance of God." [61] He writes to Titus, "Put them in mind to be subject to principalities and powers, to obey magistrates, to be ready to every good work." [62] Peter exhorts, "Submit yourselves to every ordinance of man for the Lord's sake; whether it be to the king, as supreme; or unto governors, as unto them that are sent by him for the punishment of evildoers, and for the praise of them that do well." [63] Moreover, that subjects may testify that theirs is not a hypocritical but a sincere and cordial submission, Paul teaches that they ought to pray to God for the safety and prosperity of those under whose government they live. "I exhort," he says, "that supplications, prayers, intercessions, and giving of thanks be made for all men; for kings, and for all that are in authority; that we may lead a quiet and peaceable life in all godliness and honesty." [64] Here let no man deceive him-

[61] Rom. 13:1-2.   [62] Titus 3:1.
[63] 1 Peter 2:13-14.   [64] I Tim. 2:1-2.

self. For as it is impossible to resist the magistrate without at the same time resisting God himself, though an unarmed magistrate may seem to be despised with impunity, yet God is armed to inflict exemplary vengeance on the contempt offered to himself. Under this obedience I also include the moderation which private persons ought to prescribe to themselves in relation to public affairs, that they do not, without being called upon, intermeddle with affairs of state or rashly intrude themselves into the office of magistrates, or undertake anything of a public nature. If there be anything in the public administration which requires to be corrected, let them not raise any tumults or take the business into their own hands, which ought to be all bound in this respect, but let them refer it to the cognizance of the magistrate, who is alone authorized to regulate the concerns of the public. I mean that they ought to attempt nothing without being commanded; for when they have the command of a governor, then they also are invested with public authority. For, as we are accustomed to call the counsellors of a prince "his eyes and ears," so they may not unaptly be called "his hands" whom he has commissioned to execute his commands.

XXIV. Now, as we have hitherto described a magistrate who truly answers to his title—who is the father of his country and, as the poet calls him, the pastor of his people, the guardian of peace, the protector of justice, the avenger of innocence; he would justly be deemed insane who disapproved of such a government. But, as it has happened, in almost all ages, that some princes, regardless of everything to which they ought to have directed their attention and provision, give themselves up to their pleasures in indolent exemption from every care; others, absorbed in their own interest, expose to sale all laws, privileges, rights, and judgments; others plunder the public wealth which they afterwards lavish in mad prodigality; others commit flagrant outrages, pillaging houses, violating virgins and matrons, and murdering infants; many persons cannot be persuaded that such ought to be acknowledged as princes whom, as far as possible, they ought to obey. For in such enormities and actions so completely incompatible, not only with the office of a magistrate, but with the duty of every man, they discover no appearance of the image of God, which ought to be conspicuous in a magistrate; while they perceive no vestige of that minister of God who is "not a terror to good works, but to the evil," who is sent "for the punishment of evildoers, and for the praise of them that do well"; nor recognize that governor whose dignity and authority the Scripture recommends to us. And certainly the minds of men have always been naturally disposed to hate and execrate tyrants as much as to love and reverence legitimate kings.

XXV. But, if we direct our attention to the word of God, it will carry us much farther: even to submit to the government, not only of those princes who discharge their duty to us with becoming integrity and fidelity, but of all who possess the sovereignty, even though they perform none of the duties of their function. For, though the Lord testifies that the magistrate is an eminent gift of his liberality to preserve the safety of men, and prescribes to magistrates themselves the extent of their duty, yet he at the same time declares that whatever be their characters, they have their government only from him; that those who govern for the public good are true specimens and mirrors of his beneficence; and that those who rule in an unjust and tyrannical manner are raised up by him to punish the iniquity of the people; that all equally possess that sacred majesty with which he has invested legitimate authority. I will not proceed any further till I have subjoined a few testimonies in proof of this point. It is unnecessary, however, to labor much to evince an impious king to be a judgment of God's wrath upon the world, as I have no expectation that anyone will deny it; and in this we say no more of a king than of any other robber who plunders our property, or adulterer who violates our bed, or assassin who attempts to murder us; since the Scripture enumerates all these calamities among the curses inflicted by God. But let us rather insist on the proof of that which the minds of men do not so easily admit—that a man of the worst character, and most undeserving of all honor, who holds the sovereign power, really possesses that eminent and Divine authority which the Lord has given by his word to the ministers of his justice and judgment; and, therefore, that he ought to be regarded by his subjects, as far as pertains to public obedience, with the same reverence and esteem which they would show to the best of kings, if such a one were granted to them.

XXVI. In the first place, I request my readers to observe and consider with attention what is so frequently and justly mentioned in the Scriptures—the providence and peculiar dispensation of God in distributing kingdoms and appointing whom he pleases to be kings. Daniel says, "God changeth the times and the seasons: he removeth kings and setteth up kings." [65] Again: "That the living may know that the Most High ruleth in the kingdom of men, and giveth it to whomsoever he will." [66] Passages of this kind abound throughout the Scriptures, but particularly in this prophecy. Now, the character of Nebuchadnezzar, who conquered Jerusalem, is sufficiently known: that he was an invader and depopulator of the territories of others. Yet by the mouth of Ezekiel the Lord declares that he had given him the land of Egypt, as a reward for the service which he had performed in devastating Tyre.[67] And Daniel said to him, "Thou, O king, art a king of kings; for the God of heaven hath given thee a kingdom, power, and strength, and glory; and wheresoever the children of men dwell, the beasts of the field, and the fowls of the heaven, hath he given into thine hand, and hath made thee ruler over all." [68] Again, to his grandson Belshazzar Daniel said, "The most high God gave Nebuchadnezzar thy father a kingdom, and majesty, and glory, and honor; and for the majesty that he gave him, all people, nations, and languages trembled and feared before him." [69] When we hear that Nebuchadnezzar was placed on the throne by God, let us, at

[65] Dan. 2:21.   [66] Dan. 4:17.
[67] Ezek. 24:18-20.   [68] Dan. 2:37-38.
[69] Dan. 5:18-19.

the same time, call to mind the celestial edicts which command us to fear and honor the king; and we shall not hesitate to regard the most iniquitous tyrant with the honor due to the station in which the Lord has deigned to place him. When Samuel denounced to the children of Israel what treatment they would receive from their kings, he said,

This will be the manner * of the king that shall reign over you; he will take your sons and appoint them for himself, for his chariots, and to be his horsemen, and to ear his ground, and to reap his harvest, and to make his instruments of war. And he will take your daughters to be confectionaries, and to be cooks, and to be bakers. And he will take your fields, and your vineyards, and your oliveyards, even the best of them, and give them to his servants. And he will take the tenth of your seed, and of your vineyards, and give to his officers and to his servants. And he will take your men-servants, and your maid-servants, and your goodliest young men, and your asses, and put them to his work. He will take the tenth of your sheep; and ye shall be his servants.[70]

Certainly the kings would not do all this by "right," for they were excellently instructed by the law to observe all moderation; but it was called a "right" with respect to the people who were bound to obey, and were not at liberty to resist it. It was just as if Samuel had said, The cupidity of your kings will proceed to all these outrages, which it will not be your province to restrain; nothing will remain for you but to receive their commands and to obey them.

XXVII. But the most remarkable and memorable passage of all is in the Prophecy of Jeremiah, which, though it is rather long, I shall readily quote, because it most clearly decides the whole question:

I have made the earth, the man, and the beast that are upon the ground, by my great power and by my outstretched arm, and have given it unto whom it seemed meet unto me. And now I have given all these lands into the hand of Nebuchad-

---

* [In the Latin translation, it is *jus*, right.]

[70] I Sam. 8:11-17.

nezzar, the king of Babylon, my servant. And all nations shall serve him, and his son, and his son's son, until the very time of his land come. And it shall come to pass, that the nation and kingdom which will not serve the same king of Babylon, that nation will I punish with the sword, and with the famine, and with the pestilence. Therefore serve the king of Babylon and live.[71]

We see what great obedience and honor the Lord required to be rendered to that pestilent and cruel tyrant, for no other reason than because he possessed the kingdom; and it was by the heavenly decree that he was seated on the throne of the kingdom and exalted to that regal majesty, which it was not lawful to violate. If we have this constantly present to our eyes and impressed upon our hearts, that the most iniquitous kings are placed on their thrones by the same decree by which the authority of all kings is established, those seditious thoughts will never enter our minds that a king is to be treated according to his merits, and that it is not reasonable for us to be subject to a king who does not on his part perform toward us those duties which his office requires.

XXVIII. In vain will anyone object that this was a special command given to the Israelites. For we must observe the reason upon which the Lord founds it. He says, "I have given these lands to Nebuchadnezzar; therefore serve him and live." To whomsoever, therefore, a kingdom shall evidently be given, we have no room to doubt that subjection is due to him. And as soon as he exalts any person to royal dignity, he gives us a declaration of his pleasure that he shall reign. The Scripture contains general testimonies on this subject. Solomon says, "For the transgression of a land, many are the princes thereof." [72] Job says, "He looseth the bonds of kings," or divests them of their power; "and girdeth their loins with a girdle,"[73] or restores them to their former dignity. This being admitted, nothing remains for us but to serve and live. The prophet Jeremiah likewise records another command of the Lord to his people: "Seek the peace of the city whither

71 Jer. 27:5-9, 12.   72 Prov. 28:2.   73 Job. 12:18.

I have caused you to be carried away captives, and pray unto
the Lord for it; for in the peace of it ye shall have peace." [74]
Here, we see, the Israelites, after having been stripped of all
their property, torn from their habitations, driven into exile,
and forced into a miserable servitude, were commanded to
pray for the prosperity of their conqueror; not in the same
manner in which we are all commanded to pray for our per-
secutors; but that his kingdom might be preserved in safety
and tranquility, and that they might live in prosperity under
him. Thus David, after having been already designated as
king by the ordination of God and anointed with his holy
oil, though he was unjustly persecuted by Saul, without having given him any cause of offense, nevertheless accounted
the person of his pursuer sacred because the Lord had consecrated it by the royal dignity. "And he said, The Lord forbid that I should do this thing unto my master, the Lord's
anointed, to stretch forth mine hand against him, seeing he
is the anointed of the Lord." Again: "Mine eye spared thee;
and I said, I will not put forth mine hand against my lord;
for he is the Lord's anointed." [75] Again: "Who can stretch
forth his hand against the Lord's anointed, and be guiltless?
As the Lord liveth, the Lord shall smite him; or his day shall
come to die, or he shall descend into battle, and perish. The
Lord forbid that I should stretch forth mine hand against
the Lord's anointed." [76]

XXIX. Finally, we owe these sentiments of affection and
reverence to all our rulers, whatever their characters may be;
which I the more frequently repeat, that we may learn not to
scrutinize the persons themselves, but may be satisfied with
knowing that they are invested by the will of the Lord with
that function upon which he has impressed an inviolable
majesty. But it will be said that rulers owe mutual duties to
their subjects. That I have already confessed. But he who in-
fers from this that obedience ought to be rendered to none
but just rulers is a very bad reasoner. For husbands owe mutual duties to their wives, and parents to their children. Now,

[74] Jer. 29:7.   [75] I Sam. 24:6, 11.   [76] I Sam. 26:9-11.

if husbands and parents violate their obligations; if parents conduct themselves with discouraging severity and fastidious moroseness toward their children, whom they are forbidden to provoke to wrath; [77] if husbands despise and vex their wives, whom they are commanded to love and to spare as the weaker vessels [78]—does it follow that children should be less obedient to their parents, or wives to their husbands? They are still subject even to those who are wicked and unkind. As it is incumbent on all, not to inquire into the duties of one another, but to confine their attention respectively to their own, this consideration ought particularly to be regarded by those who are subject to the authority of others. Wherefore, if we are inhumanly harassed by a cruel prince; if we are rapaciously plundered by an avaricious or luxurious one; if we are neglected by an indolent one; or if we are persecuted, on account of piety, by an impious and sacrilegious one—let us first call to mind our transgressions against God, which he undoubtedly chastises by these scourges. Thus our impatience will be restrained by humility. Let us, in the next place, consider that it is not our province to remedy these evils, and that nothing remains for us but to implore the aid of the Lord, in whose hand are the hearts of kings and the revolutions of kingdoms. It is "God" who "standeth in the congregation of the mighty," and "judgeth among the gods"; [79] whose presence shall confound and crush all kings and judges of the earth who shall not have kissed his Son; [80] "that decree unrighteous decrees, to turn aside the needy from judgment, and to take away the right from the poor, that widows may be their prey, and that they may rob the fatherless." [81]

XXX. And here is displayed his wonderful goodness and power and providence; for sometimes he raises up some of his servants as public avengers and arms them with his commission to punish unrighteous domination, and to deliver

[77] Ephes. 6:1. Col. 3:21.
[79] Psalm 82:1.
[81] Isaiah 10:1-2.

[78] Ephes. 5:25. I Pet. 3:7.
[80] Psalm 2:10-12.

from their distressing calamities a people who have been unjustly oppressed; sometimes he accomplishes this end by the
fury of men who meditate and attempt something altogether
different. Thus he liberated the people of Israel from the
tyranny of Pharaoh by Moses; from the oppression of Chusan
by Othniel; and from other yokes by other kings and judges.
Thus he subdued the pride of Tyre by the Egyptians; the
insolence of the Egyptians by the Assyrians; the haughtiness
of the Assyrians by the Chaldeans; the confidence of Babylon by the Medes and Persians, after Cyrus had subjugated
the Medes. The ingratitude of the kings of Israel and Judah
and their impious rebellion, notwithstanding his numerous
favors, he repressed and punished sometimes by the Assyrians,
sometimes by the Babylonians. These were all the execution-
ers of his vengeance, but not all in the same manner. The
former, when they were called forth to the performance of
such acts by a legitimate commission from God, in taking
arms against kings, were not chargeable with the least violation of that majesty with which kings are invested by the
ordination of God; but, being armed with authority from
Heaven, they punished an inferior power by a superior one,
as it is lawful for kings to punish their inferior officers. The
latter, though they were guided by the hand of God in such
directions as he pleased, and performed his work without being conscious of it, nevertheless contemplated in their hearts
nothing but evil.

XXXI. But whatever opinion be formed of the acts of men,
yet the Lord equally executed his work by them when he
broke the sanguinary scepters of insolent kings and over-
turned tyrannical governments. Let princes hear and fear.
But, in the meanwhile, it behooves us to use the greatest caution, that we do not despise or violate that authority of magistrates which is entitled to the greatest veneration, which
God has established by the most solemn commands, even
though it reside in those who are most unworthy of it, and
who, as far as in them lies, pollute it by their iniquity. For
though the correction of tyrannical domination is the ven-

geance of God, we are not, therefore, to conclude that it is committed to us who have received no other command than to obey and suffer. This observation I always apply to private persons. For if there be, in the present day, any magistrates appointed for the protection of the people and the moderation of the power of kings, such as were, in ancient times, the Ephori, who were a check upon the kings among the Lacedaemonians, or the popular tribunes upon the consuls among the Romans, or the Demarchi upon the senate among the Athenians; or with power such as perhaps is now possessed by the three estates in every kingdom when they are assembled; I am so far from prohibiting them, in the discharge of their duty, to oppose the violence or cruelty of kings that I affirm that if they connive at kings in their oppression of their people, such forbearance involves the most nefarious perfidy because they fraudulently betray the liberty of the people, of which they know that they have been appointed protectors by the ordination of God.

XXXII. But in the obedience which we have shown to be due to the authority of governors, it is always necessary to make one exception, and that is entitled to our first attention —that it do not seduce us from obedience to him to whose will the desires of all kings ought to be subject, to whose decrees all their commands ought to yield, to whose majesty all their scepters ought to submit. And, indeed, how preposterous it would be for us, with a view to satisfy men, to incur the displeasure of him on whose account we yield obedience to men! The Lord, therefore, is the King of kings; who, when he has opened his sacred mouth, is to be heard alone, above all, for all, and before all; in the next place, we are subject to those men who preside over us, but no otherwise than in him. If they command anything against him, it ought not to have the least attention, nor, in this case, ought we to pay any regard to all that dignity attached to magistrates, to which no injury is done when it is subjected to the unrivaled and supreme power of God. On this principle Daniel denied that he had committed any crime against the king in disobeying his impious decree; [82] because the king had exceeded the limits of his office, and had not only done an injury to men, but, by raising his arm against God, had degraded his own authority. On the other hand, the Israelites are condemned for having been too submissive to the impious edict of their king. For when Jeroboam had made his golden calves, in compliance with his will, they deserted the temple of God and revolted to new superstitions. Their posterity conformed to the decrees of their idolatrous kings with the same facility. The prophet severely condemns them for having "willingly walked after the commandment"; [83] so far is any praise from being due to the pretext of humility with which courtly flatterers excuse themselves and deceive the unwary, when they deny that it is lawful for them to refuse compliance with any command of their kings, as if God had resigned his right to mortal men when he made them rulers of mankind, or as if earthly power were diminished by being subordinated to its author before whom even the principalities of heaven tremble with awe. I know what great and present danger awaits this constancy, for kings cannot bear to be disregarded without the greatest indignation; and "the wrath of a king," says Solomon, "is as messengers of death." [84] But since this edict has been proclaimed by that celestial herald, Peter, "We ought to obey God rather than men," [85]—let us console ourselves with this thought, that we truly perform the obedience which God requires of us when we suffer anything rather than deviate from piety. And that our hearts may not fail us, Paul stimulates us with another consideration—that Christ has redeemed us at the immense price which our redemption cost him, that we may not be submissive to the corrupt desires of men, much less be slaves to their impiety. [86]

[82] Dan. 6:22.
[83] Hos. 5:11.
[84] Prov. 16:14.
[85] Acts 5:29.
[86] I Cor. 7:23.

Commentaries on the Epistle to the Romans

Selections

CHAPTER XIII

1. Let every soul be subject unto the higher powers. For there is no power but of God: the powers that be are ordained of God.

2. Whosoever therefore resisteth the power, resisteth the ordinance of God; and they that resist shall receive to themselves damnation.

1. "Let every soul," etc. Inasmuch as he so carefully handles this subject, in connection with what forms the Christian life, it appears that he was constrained to do so by some great necessity which existed especially in that age, though the preaching of the Gospel at all times renders this necessary. There are indeed always some tumultuous spirits who believe that the kingdom of Christ cannot be sufficiently elevated unless all earthly powers be abolished, and that they cannot enjoy the liberty given by him except they shake off every yoke of human subjection. This error, however, possessed the minds of the Jews above all others; for it seemed to them disgraceful that the offspring of Abraham, whose kingdom flourished before the Redeemer's coming, should now, after his appearance, continue in submission to another power. There was also another thing which alienated the Jews no less than the Gentiles from their rulers, because they all not only hated piety, but also persecuted religion with the most hostile feelings. Hence it seemed unreasonable to acknowledge them for legitimate princes and rulers who were attempting to take away the kingdom from Christ, the only Lord of heaven and earth.

By these reasons, as it is probable, Paul was induced to establish, with greater care than usual, the authority of magistrates, and first he lays down a general precept which briefly includes what he afterwards says; secondly, he subjoins an exposition and a proof of his precept.

He calls them the *higher powers,* not the supreme, who possess the chief authority, but such as excel other men. Magistrates are then thus called with regard to their subjects, and not as compared with each other. And it seems indeed to me that the Apostle intended by this word to take away the frivolous curiosity of men, who are wont often to inquire by what right they who rule have obtained their authority; but it ought to be enough for us that they *do rule;* for they have not ascended by their own power into this high station, but have been placed there by the Lord's hand. And by mentioning *every soul,* he removes every exception, lest anyone should claim an immunity from the common duty of obedience.

"For there is no power," etc. The reason why we ought to be subject to magistrates is because they are constituted by God's ordination. For since it pleases God thus to govern the world, he who attempts to invert the order of God, and thus to resist God himself, despises his power; since to despise the providence of him who is the founder of civil power is to carry on war with him. Understand further that powers are from God, not as pestilence and famine and wars and other visitations for sin are said to be from him, but because he has appointed them for the legitimate and just government of the world. For though tyrannies and unjust exercise of power, as they are full of disorder, are not an ordained government, yet the right of government is ordained by God for the well-being of mankind. As it is lawful to repel wars and to seek remedies for other evils, hence the Apostle commands us willingly and cheerfully to respect and honor the right and authority of magistrates, as useful to men: for the punishment which God inflicts on men for their sins, we cannot properly call ordinations, but they are the means which he designedly appoints for the preservation of legitimate order.

2. "And they who resist," etc. As no one can resist God but to his own ruin, he threatens that they shall not be unpunished who in this respect oppose the providence of God. Let us then beware lest we incur this denunciation. And by "judgment," I understand not only the punishment which is in-

flicted by the magistrate, as though he had only said that they would be justly punished who resisted authority, but also the vengeance of God, however it may at length be executed; for he teaches us in general what end awaits those who contend with God.

3. For rulers are not a terror to good works, but to the evil. Wilt thou then not be afraid of the power? Do that which is good, and thou shalt have praise of the same;

4. For he is the minister of God to thee for good. But if thou do that which is evil, be afraid; for he beareth not the sword in vain: for he is the minister of God, a revenger to execute wrath upon him that doeth evil.

3. "For princes," etc. He now commends to us obedience to princes on the ground of utiltiy; for the causative *"for"* is to be referred to the first proposition, and not to the last verse. Now the utility is this—that the Lord has designed in this way to provide for the tranquility of the good, and to restrain the waywardness of the wicked, by which two things the safety of mankind is secured; for except the fury of the wicked be resisted, and the innocent be protected from their violence, all things would come to an entire confusion. Since then this is the only remedy by which mankind can be preserved from destruction, it ought to be carefully observed by us unless we wish to avow ourselves as the public enemies of the human race.

And he adds, "Wilt not thou then fear the power? Do good." By this he intimates that there is no reason why we should dislike the magistrate if indeed we are good; nay, that it is an implied proof of an evil conscience, and of one that is devising some mischief, when anyone wishes to shake off or to remove from himself this yoke. But he speaks here of the true and, as it were, of the native duty of the magistrate, from which however they who hold power often degenerate; yet the obedience due to princes ought to be rendered to them. For since a wicked prince is the Lord's scourge to punish the sins of the people, let us remember that it happens through our fault that this excellent blessing of God is turned into a curse.

Let us then continue to honor the good appointment of God, which may be easily done provided we impute to ourselves whatever evil may accompany it. Hence he teaches us here the end for which magistrates are instituted by the Lord; the happy effects of which would always appear were not so noble and salutary an institution marred through our fault. At the same time, princes do never so far abuse their power, by harassing the good and innocent, that they do not retain in their tyranny some kind of just government: there can then be no tyranny which does not in some respects assist in consolidating the society of men.

He has here noticed two things which even philosophers have considered as making a part of a well-ordered administration of a commonwealth—that is, rewards for the good, and punishment for the wicked. The word "praise" has here, after the Hebrew manner, a wide meaning.

4. "For he is God's minister for good," etc. Magistrates may hence learn what their vocation is, for they are not to rule for their own interest, but for the public good; nor are they endued with unbridled power, but what is restricted to the well-being of their subjects; in short, they are responsible to God and to men in the exercise of their power. For as they are deputed by God and do his business, they must give an account to him: and then the ministration which God has committed to them has a regard to the subjects, they are therefore debtors also to them. And private men are reminded that it is through the divine goodness that they are defended by the sword of princes against injuries done by the wicked.

"For they bear not the sword in vain," etc. It is another part of the office of magistrates that they ought forcibly to repress the waywardness of evil men, who do not willingly suffer themselves to be governed by laws, and to inflict such punishment on their offenses as God's judgment requires; for he expressly declares that they are armed with the sword, not for an empty show, but that they may smite evildoers.

And then he says, "An avenger, to *execute* wrath," etc. This is the same as if it had been said that he is an executioner of God's wrath; and this he shows himself to be by having the sword, which the Lord has delivered into his hand. This is a remarkable passage for the purpose of proving the right of the sword; for if the Lord, by arming the magistrate, has also committed to him the use of the sword, whenever he visits the guilty with death, by executing God's vengeance, he obeys his commands. Contend then do they with God who think it unlawful to shed the blood of wicked men.

5. Wherefore ye must needs be subject, not only for wrath, but also for conscience' sake.

5. *It is therefore necessary, etc.* What he had at first commanded as to the rendering of obedience to magistrates, he now briefly repeats, but with some addition, and that is—that we ought to obey them, not only on the ground of necessity arising from man, but that we thereby obey God; for by *wrath* he means the punishment which the magistrates inflict for the contempt of their dignity; as though he had said, "We must not only obey because we cannot with impunity resist the powerful and those armed with authority, as injuries are wont to be borne with which cannot be repelled; but we ought to obey willingly, as conscience through God's word thus binds us." Though then the magistrate were disarmed, so that we could with impunity provoke and despise him, yet such a thing ought to be no more attempted than if we were to see punishment suspended over us; for it belongs not to a private individual to take away authority from him whom the Lord has in power set over us. This whole discourse is concerning civil government; it is therefore to no purpose that they who would exercise dominion over consciences do hence attempt to establish their sacrilegious tyranny.

Commentaries on Daniel

Selections

DEDICATORY EPISTLE

JOHN CALVIN

TO ALL THE PIOUS WORSHIPPERS OF GOD WHO DESIRE THE KINGDOM OF CHRIST TO BE RIGHTLY CONSTITUTED IN FRANCE

HEALTH

ALTHOUGH I have been absent these twenty-six years, with little regret, from that native land which I own in common with yourselves, and whose agreeable climate attracts many foreigners from the most distant quarters of the world, yet it would be in no degree pleasing or desirable to me to dwell in a region from which the truth of God, pure religion, and the doctrine of eternal salvation are banished, and the very kingdom of Christ laid prostrate! Hence I have no desire to return to it; yet it would be neither in accordance with human nor divine obligation to forget the people from which I am sprung, and to put away all regard for their welfare. I think I have given some strong proofs how seriously and ardently I desire to benefit my fellow countrymen, to whom perhaps my absence has been useful, in enabling them to reap the greater profit from my studies. And the contemplation of this advantage has not only deprived my banishment of its sting, but has rendered it even pleasant and joyful.

Since, therefore, throughout the whole of this period I have publicly endeavored to benefit *the inhabitants of France,* and have never ceased privately to rouse the torpid, to stimulate the sluggish, to animate the trembling, and to encourage the doubtful and the wavering to perseverance, I must now strive to the utmost that my duty toward them may not fail at a period so urgent and so pressing. A most excellent opportunity has been providentially afforded to me; for in publishing

the "Lectures" which contain my interpretation of the proph-
ecies of Daniel, I have the very best occasion of showing you,
beloved brethren, in this mirror, how God proves the faith
of his people in these days by various trials, and how with
wonderful wisdom he has taken care to strengthen their minds
by ancient examples, that they should never be weakened by
the concussion of the severest storms and tempests; or at least,
if they should totter at all, that they should never finally
fall away. For although the servants of God are required to
run in a course impeded by many obstacles, yet whoever dili-
gently reads this book will find in it whatever is needed by
a voluntary and active runner to guide him from the start-
ing post to the goal; while good and strenuous wrestlers will
experimentally acknowledge that they have been sufficiently
prepared for the contest.

First of all, a very mournful and yet profitable history will
be recorded for us, in the exile of Daniel and his companions
while the kingdom and priesthood were still standing, as if
God, through ignominy and shame, would devote the choicest
flower of his elect people to extreme calamity. For what, at
first, is more unbecoming than that youths endued with almost angelic virtues should be the slaves and captives of a
proud conqueror, when the most wicked and abandoned despisers of God remained at home in perfect safety? Was this
the reward of a pious and innocent life, that, while the impious were sweetly flattering themselves through their escape
from punishment, the saints should pay the penalty which
they had deserved? Here, then, we observe, as in a living pic-
ture, that when God spares and even indulges the wicked for
a time, he proves his servants like gold and silver, so that we
ought not to consider it a grievance to be thrown into the
furnace of trial, while profane men enjoy the calmness of
repose.

Secondly, we have here an example of most manly prudence
and of singular consistency, united with a magnanimity truly
heroic. When pious youths of a tender age are tempted by the
enticements of a court, they not only overcome the tempta-

tions presented to them by their temperance, but perceive themselves cunningly enticed to depart by degrees from the sincere worship of God; and then, when they have extricated themselves from the snares of the devil, they boldly and freely despise all poison-stained honor, at the imminent risk of instant death. A more cruel and formidable contest will follow when the companions of Daniel, as a memorable example of incredible constancy, are never turned aside by atrocious threats to pollute themselves by adoring the Image, and are at length prepared to vindicate the pure worship of God, not only with their blood, but in defiance of a horrible torture set before their eyes. Thus the goodness of God shines forth at the close of this tragedy, and tends in no slight degree to arm us with invincible confidence.

A similar contest and victory of Daniel himself will be added—when he preferred to be cast among savage lions to desisting from the open profession of his faith three times a day lest by perfidious dissembling he should prostitute the Sacred Name of God to the jests of the impious. Thus he was wonderfully drawn out of the pit which was all but his grave, and triumphed over Satan and his faction. Here philosophers do not come before us skillfully disputing about the virtues peacefully in the shade; but the indefatigable constancy of holy men in the pursuit of piety invites us with a loud voice to imitate them. Therefore, unless we are altogether unteachable, we ought to learn from these masters, if Satan lays the snares of flattery for us, to be prudent and cautious that we are not entangled in them; and if he attacks us violently, to oppose all his assaults by a fearless contempt of death and of all evils. Should anyone object that the examples of either kind of deliverance which we have mentioned are rare, I confess indeed that God does not always stretch forth his hand from heaven in the same way to preserve his people; but it ought to satisfy us that he has promised that he will be a faithful guardian of our life as often as we are harassed by any trouble. We cannot be exposed to the power of the impious without his restraining their furious and turbulent plots against us, according to his pleasure. And we must not look at the results alone, but observe how courageously holy men devoted themselves to death for the vindication of God's glory; and although they were snatched away from it, yet their willing alacrity in offering themselves as victims is in no degree less deserving of praise.

. . . .

LECTURE TWENTY-EIGHTH

We said yesterday that the nobles who laid snares against Daniel were inspired with great fury when they dared to dictate to the king the edict recorded by Daniel. It was an intolerable sacrilege thus to deprive all the deities of their honor, yet he subscribed the edict, as we shall afterwards see, and thus put to the test the obedience of his people whom he had lately reduced under the yoke by the help of his son-in-law. There is no doubt of his wish to subdue the Chaldeans, who up to that time had been masters; and we know how ferocity springs from the possession of authority. Since then the Chaldeans had formerly reigned so far and wide, it was difficult to tame them and render them submissive, especially when they found themselves the slaves of those who had previously been their rivals. We know how many contests there were between them and the Medes; and although they were subdued in war, their spirits were not yet in subjection; hence Darius desired to prove their obedience, and this reason induced him to give his consent. He does not purposely provoke the anger of the gods, but through respect for the men, he forgets the deities and substitutes himself in the place of the gods, as if it was in his power to attract the authority of heaven to himself! This, as I have said, was a grievous sacrilege. If anyone could enter into the hearts of kings, he would find scarcely one in a hundred who does not despise everything divine. Although they confess themselves to enjoy their thrones by the grace of God, as we have previously remarked, yet they wish to be adored in his stead. We now see how easily flatterers persuade kings to do whatever appears likely to extol their magnificence. It follows:

8. Now, O king, establish the decree, and sign the writing, that it be not changed, according to the law of the Medes and Persians, which altereth not.

9. Wherefore king Darius signed the writing and the decree.

Here, as I have said, it is sufficiently apparent how inclined to fallacies are the minds of kings when they think they can benefit themselves and increase their own dignity. For the king did not dispute long with his nobles but subscribed the edict; for he thought it might prove useful to himself and his successors if he found the Chaldeans obedient to himself and rather prepared to deny the existence of every god than to refuse whatever he commanded! As to the use of the word, some translate *asra* by "writing," deriving it from "to cut in," as we know that all laws were formerly graven on tablets of brass; but I interpret it more simply of their seeking from the king a signature of the writing, that is, he was to sign the edict after it was written. *Which cannot be changed,* they say—meaning the edict is unchangeable and inviolable, *according to the law of the Medes and Persians, which does not pass away*—that is, which does not vanish, as also Christ says, Heaven and earth shall pass away, but my words shall not pass away, or shall never become vain. (Matt. xxiv. 35; Mark xiii. 31.) As to his joining the Medes with the Persians, this arises from what we said before, since Cyrus and Darius reigned in common as colleagues. Greater dignity was granted to Darius, while the power was in the hands of Cyrus; besides, without controversy, his sons were heirs of either kingdom and of the Monarchy of the East, unless when they began to make war on each other. When they say the law of the Medes and Persians *is immutable,* this is worthy of praise in laws, and sanctions their authority; thus they are strong and obtain their full effect. When laws are variable, many are necessarily injured, and no private interest is stable unless the law be without variation; besides, when there is a liberty of changing laws, license succeeds in place of justice. For those who possess the supreme power, if corrupted by gifts, promulgate first one edict and then another. Thus justice cannot flourish where change in the laws allows of so much license. But, at the same time, kings ought prudently to consider lest they promulgate any edict or law without grave and mature deliberation; and secondly, kings ought to be careful lest they be counteracted by cunning and artful plots, to which they are often liable. Hence constancy is praiseworthy in kings and their edicts, if only they are preceded by prudence and equity. But we shall immediately see how foolishly kings affect the fame of consistency, and how their obstinacy utterly perverts justice. But we shall see this directly in its own place.

. . . .

LECTURE TWENTY-NINTH

We began yesterday to explain Daniel's narrative of the calumny invented against him before King Darius. The nobles of the kingdom, as we have said, used cunning in their interview with the king; because if they had begun with Daniel, the king might have broken his word. But they dwell upon the royal decree—they show the imminence of the danger unless the authority of all the king's decrees was upheld. By this artifice we see how they obtained their object; for the king confirms their assertion respecting the wickedness of rendering abortive what had been promulgated in the king's name. For kings are pleased with their own greatness and wish their own pleasure to be treated as an oracle. That edict was detestable and impious by which Darius forbade entreaties to be offered to any deity, yet he wished it to remain in force lest his majesty should be despised by his subjects. Meanwhile, he does not perceive the consequences which

must ensue. Hence we are taught by this example that no virtue is so rare in kings as moderation, and yet none is more
necessary; for the more they have in their power, the more
it becomes them to be cautious lest they indulge their lusts,
while they think it lawful to desire whatever pleases them.
It now follows:

*13. Then answered they, and said before the king, That Daniel, which
is of the children of the captivity of Judah, regardeth not thee, O king,
nor the decree that thou hast signed, but maketh his petition three times
a day.*

Now, when Daniel's calumniators see that King Darius had
no wish to defend his cause, they open up more freely what
they had previously concealed; for, as we have said, if they
had openly accused Daniel, their accusation could have been
instantly and completely refuted; but after this sentiment had
been expressed to the king, their statement is final, since by
the laws of the Medes and Persians a king's decree ought to
be self-acting; hence, after this is accomplished, they then
come to the person. "Daniel," say they, "one of the captives
of Judah, has not obeyed thy will, O king, nor the decree
which thou hast signed." By saying, "Daniel, one of the Jewish captives," they doubtless intended to magnify his crime
and to render him odious. For if any Chaldean had dared to
despise the king's edict, his rashness would not have been
excused. But now when Daniel, who was lately a slave and a
Chaldean captive, dares to despise the king's command, who
reigned over Chaldea by the right of conquest, this seemed
less tolerable still. The effect is the same as if they had said,
"He was lately a captive among thy slaves; thou art supreme
lord, and his masters to whom he was subject are under thy
yoke, because thou art their conqueror; he is but a captive
and a stranger, a mere slave, and yet he rebels against thee!"
We see then how they desired to poison the king's mind
against him by this allusion, *He is one of the captives!* The
words are very harmless in themselves, but they endeavor to
sting their monarch in every way, and to stir up his wrath

against Daniel. "He does not direct his mind to thee, O king"; that is, he does not reflect upon who you are, and thus he despises thy majesty and *the edict which thou hast signed.* This is another enlargement: *Daniel,* therefore, *did not direct his mind either to thee or to thy edict;* and wilt thou bear this? Next, they recite the deed itself—*he prays three times a day.* This would have been the simple narrative: Daniel has not obeyed thy command in praying to his own God; but, as I have said, they exaggerate his crime by accusing him of pride, contempt, and insolence. We see, therefore, by what artifices Daniel was oppressed by these malicious men. It now follows:

14. *Then the king, when he heard these words, was sore displeased with himself and set his heart on Daniel to deliver him; and he laboured till the going down of the sun to deliver him.*

15. *Then these men assembled unto the king, and said unto the king, Know, O king, that the law of the Medes and Persians is, That no decree nor statute which the king establisheth may be changed.*

In the first place, Daniel recites that the king was disturbed when he perceived the malice of his nobles which had formerly escaped him; for their intention and their object had never occurred to him; he perceives himself deceived and entrapped, and hence he is disturbed. Here again we are taught how cautiously kings ought to avoid depraved counsels, since they are besieged on every side by perfidious men, whose only object is to gain by their false representations, and to oppress their enemies and those from whom they hope for booty or who may favor their evil courses. Because so many snares surround kings, they ought to be the more cautious in providing against cunning. They are too late in acknowledging themselves to have been overreached, when no remedy is left, partly through fear and partly through wishing to consult their own credit; and they prefer offending God to suffering any outward disrespect from men. Since, therefore, kings consider their own honor so sacred, they persevere in their evil undertakings, even when their conscience accuses them, and even if justice itself were to appear visibly before them; yet this restraint would not be sufficient to withhold them when ambition urges them in the opposite direction and they are unwilling to lose the slightest portion of their reputation among men. The case of Darius supplies us with an example of this kind.

First of all, it is said, "He was sorrowful when he heard these words, and was anxious till the setting of the sun about the way of snatching Daniel from death." He wished this to be done, if his own honor were sound and safe, and his nobles were satisfied. But, on the one side, he fears disunion if his nobles should conspire to produce disturbance, and, on the other side, he is moved by a foolish fear, because he does not wish to incur the charge of levity which awaited him, and hence he is vanquished and obeys the lusts of the wicked. Although, therefore, he labored till the setting of the sun to free Daniel, yet that perverse shame prevailed of which I have spoken, and then the fear of dissension. For when we do not lean upon God's help, we are always compelled to vacillate, although anxious to be honestly affected. Thus Pilate wished to liberate Christ, but was terrified by the threats of the people when they denounced against him the displeasure of Caesar (John xix. 12). And no wonder, since faith is alone a certain and fixed prop on which we may lean while fearlessly discharging our duty, and thus overcome all fears. But when we want confidence, we are, as I have said, sure to be changeable. Hence Darius, through fear of a conspiracy of his nobles against himself, permitted Daniel to be an innocent sufferer from their cruelty. Then that false shame is added which I have mentioned, because he was unwilling to appear without consideration, by suddenly revoking his own edict, as it was a law with the Medes and Persians that whatever proceeded from kings was inviolable! Daniel now states this. He says, "those men assembled together"; when they saw the king hesitate and doubt, they became fierce and contentious with him. When it is said they meet together, this relates to their inspiring him with fear. They say, "Know, O king!" He knew it well enough, and they need not instruct him in any un-known matter, but they treat him in a threatening manner. "What! dost thou not see how utterly the royal name will be hereafter deprived of its authority if he violates thine edict with impunity? Will you thus permit yourself to become a laughingstock?" Finally, they intimate that he would not be king unless he revenged the insult offered him by Daniel in neglecting his commandment. "Know, therefore, O king, that the Persians and Medes"—he was himself king of the Medes, but it is just as if they said, "What kind of rumor will be spread through all thy subject provinces; for thou knowest how far this prevails among the Medes and Persians—the king must not change his edict. If, therefore, thou shouldst set such an example, will not all thy subjects instantly rise against thee, and wilt thou not be contemptible to them?" We see, then, how the satraps rage against their king and frighten him from any change of counsel. And they also join the edict with the statute which the king had resolved upon, with the view of impressing upon him the necessity of not changing a single decree which he had often and repeatedly sanctioned. It fol-lows:

16. *Then the king commanded, and they brought Daniel, and cast* him *into the den of lions. Now the king spake, and said unto Daniel, Thy God, whom thou servest continually, he will deliver thee.*

The king, as we have said, frightened by the denunciation of the nobles, condemns Daniel to death. And hence we gather the reward which kings deserve in reference to their pride, when they are compelled to submit with servility to their flat-terers. How was Darius deceived by the cunning of his nobles! For he thought his authority would be strengthened by put-ting the obedience of all men to this test of refusing all prayer to any god or man for a whole month. He thought he should become superior to both gods and men, if all his subjects really manifested obedience of this kind. We now see how obstinately the nobles rise against him, and denounce ulti-mate revolt unless he obey them. We see that when kings

take too much upon themselves, how they are exposed to infamy and become the veriest slaves of their own servants! This
is common enough with earthly princes; those who possess
their influence and favor applaud them in all things and even
adore them; they offer every kind of flattery which can pro-
pitiate their favor; but, meanwhile, what freedom do their
idols enjoy? They do not allow them any authority, nor any
intercourse with the best and most faithful friends, while they
are watched by their own guards. Lastly, if they are compared
with the wretches who are confined in the closest dungeon,
not one who is thrust down into the deepest pit and watched
by three or four guards, is not freer than kings themselves!
But, as I have said, this is God's most just vengeance; since,
when they cannot contain themselves in the ordinary rank
and station of men, but wish to penetrate the clouds and become on a level with God, they necessarily become a laughingstock. Hence they become slaves of all their attendants and
dare not utter anything with freedom, and are without friends,
and are afraid to summon their subjects to their presence, and
to intrust either one or another with their wishes. Thus slaves
rule the kingdoms of the world, because kings assume su-
periority to mortals. King Darius is an instance of this when
he sent for Daniel and commanded him to be thrown into the
den of lions; his nobles force this from him, and he unwill-
ingly obeys them. But we should notice the reason. He had
lately forgotten his own mortality, he had desired to deprive
the Almighty of his sway, and as it were to drag him down
from heaven! For if God remains in heaven, men must pray
to him; but Darius forbade anyone from even daring to utter
a prayer; hence as far as he could he deprived the Almighty
of his power. Now he is compelled to obey his own subjects,
although they exercise an almost disgraceful tyranny over
him.

Daniel now adds—"the king said this to him, Thy God,
whom thou servest, or worshippest, faithfully, he will deliver
thee!" This word may be read in the optative mood, as we
have said. There is no doubt that Darius really wished this;

but it may mean, Thy God whom thou worshippest will deliver thee—as if he had said, "Already I am not my own master, I am here tossed about by the blast of a tempest; my nobles compel me to this deed against my will; I, therefore, now resign thee and thy life to God, because it is not in my power to deliver thee"; as if this excuse lightened his own crime by transferring to God the power of preserving Daniel. This reason causes some to praise the piety of King Darius; but as I confess his clemency and humanity to be manifest in this speech, so it is clear that he had not a grain of piety when he thus wished to adorn himself in the spoils of deity! For although the superstitious do not seriously fear God, yet they are restrained by some dread of him; but he here wished to reduce the whole divinity to nothing. What sort of piety was this? The clemency of Darius may therefore be praised, but his sacrilegious pride can by no means be excused. Then, why did he act so humanely toward Daniel? Because he had found him a faithful servant, and the regard which rendered him merciful arose from this peculiarity. He would not have manifested the same disposition toward others. If a hundred or a thousand Jews had been dragged before his tribunal, he would carelessly have condemned them all because they had disobeyed the edict! Hence he was obstinately impious and cruel. He spared Daniel for his own private advantage, and thus embraced him with his favor; but in praising his humanity, we do not perceive any sign of piety in him. But he says, "the God whom thou worshippest, he will deliver thee," because he had formerly known Daniel's prophecy concerning the destruction of the Chaldean monarchy; hence he is convinced how Israel's God is conscious of all things and rules everything by his will; yet, in the meantime, he neither worships him nor suffers others to do so; for as far as he could he had excluded God from his own rights. In thus attributing to God the power of delivering him, he does not act cordially; and hence his impiety is the more detestable when he deprives God of his rights while he confesses him to be the true and only one endued with supreme power; and though he is but dust and ashes, yet he substitutes himself in his place! It now follows:

17. And a stone was brought, and laid upon the mouth of the den; and the king sealed it with his own signet, and with the signet of his lords; that the purpose might not be changed concerning Daniel.

There is no doubt that God's counsel provided that the nobles should seal the stone with their own rings, and thus close the mouth of the cave and render the miracle more illustrious. For when the king approached on the morrow, the rings were all entire and the seals all unbroken. Thus the preservation of this servant of God was manifest by the aid of heaven and not by the art of men. Hence we see how boldly the king's nobles had compelled him to perform their pleasure. For he might seem deprived of all royal power when he delivered up to them a subject dear and faithful to himself, and ordered him to be thrown into the lions' den. They are not content with this compliance of the king; they extort another point from him—the closing up of the mouth of the cave; and then they all seal the stone lest anyone should release Daniel. We see, then, when once liberty has been snatched away, all is over, especially when anyone has become a slave by his own faults, and has attached himself to the counsels of the ungodly. For, at first, such slavery will not prevail as to induce a man to do everything which he is ordered, since he seems to be free; but when he has given himself up to such slavery as I have described, he is compelled to transgress not once or twice, but constantly and without ceasing. For example, if anyone swerves from his duty through either the fear of man or flattery or any other depraved affection, he will grant various things, not only when asked, but when urgently compelled. But when he has once submitted to the loss of freedom, he will be compelled, as I have already said, to consent to the most shameful deeds at the nod of anyone. If any teacher or pastor of the Church should turn from the right path through the influence of ambition, the author of his declension will come to him again and say,

What! do you dare to refuse me? Did I not obtain from you, yesterday or the day before, whatever I wished? Thus he will be compelled to transgress a second time in favor of the person to whom he has joined himself, and will also be forced to repeat the transgression continually. Thus princes also who are not free agents through being under the tyranny of others, if they permit themselves to be overcome contrary to their conscience, lay aside all their authority and are drawn aside in all directions by the will of their subjects. This example, then, is proposed to us in the case of King Darius, who after inflicting unjust punishment upon Daniel adds this, "He must be enclosed in the cave," and then, "the stone must be sealed" —and for what object?—"lest the doom should be changed"; meaning, he did not dare to attempt anything in Daniel's favor. We see, then, how the king submitted to the greatest disgrace because his nobles had no confidence in him; they refused to trust him when he ordered Daniel to be thrown into the lions' den, but they exacted a guarantee against his liberation, and would not suffer him to attempt anything.

. . . .

LECTURE THIRTIETH

. . . .

. . . We know how earthly empires are constituted by God, only on the condition that he deprives himself of nothing, but shines forth alone, and all magistrates must be set in regular order, and every authority in existence must be subject to his glory. Since, therefore, Daniel could not obey the king's edict without denying God, as we have previously seen, he did not transgress against the king by constantly persevering in that exercise of piety to which he had been accustomed, and by calling on his God three times a day. To make this the more evident, we must remember that passage of Peter, "Fear God, honor the king" (1 Pet. ii. 17). The two commands are connected together, and cannot be separated from one another. The fear of God ought to precede, that kings may obtain their authority. For if anyone begins his reverence of an earthly prince by rejecting that of God, he will act preposterously, since this is a complete perversion of the order of nature. Then let God be feared in the first place, and earthly princes will obtain their authority, if only God shines forth, as I have already said. Daniel, therefore, here defends himself with justice, since *he had not committed any crime against the king;* for he was compelled to obey the command of God, and he neglected what the king had ordered in opposition to it. For earthly princes lay aside all their power when they rise up against God, and are unworthy of being reckoned in the number of mankind. We ought rather utterly to defy than to obey them whenever they are so restive and wish to spoil God of his rights, and, as it were, to seize upon his throne and draw him down from heaven. Now, therefore, we understand the sense of this passage.